Financial Freedom

More Than Being Debt Free

by
**Patrick Clements
and Dave Gerig**

D1261917

Published by VMI Publishers
P.O. Box 1676, Sisters, Oregon 97759

Unless otherwise indicated, scripture quotations are taken from the New
International Version (NIV), copyright 1973, 1978, 1979 by International Bible
Society. Scripture quotations marked NKJV are taken from the New King
James Version copyright 1979 by Thomas Nelson Publishers. Scripture quota-
tions marked NLT are taken from the New Living Translation, copyright 1996
by Tyndale House Publishers. Scriptures marked "The Message" are taken
from The Message, The Bible in Contemporary Language, by Eugene H.
Peterson, copyright 2002 NavPress Publisher.

Book Jacket Design by Clint Davis

Printed in the United States of America

ISBN 0-9712311-4-1

DEDICATION

To my wife, Connie. She is my true love, best friend, and life partner and has unselfishly offered her encouragement and support to me throughout 34 years of marriage.

———

ACKNOWLEDGEMENTS

I would like to offer special thanks to the following individuals for the time and energy they have given to the completion of this project.

- to Bill Carmichael, president of VMI Publishers, for his friendship and encouragement to me to put my thoughts on paper, and then his willingness to publish the end result;

- to my son, Ned Clements, who lent his publishing expertise to the process;

- to Mary Schulz, my assistant, for coordinating the project and putting all the pieces into one cohesive package;

- and to my mother, who demonstrated by her example to me the value of faithful stewardship.

———

CONTENTS

Introduction

THE JOURNEY TO BECOMING A STEWARD

If you are reading this, then you are likely hoping to find some solutions to your financial situation. Regardless of where you are on your financial journey, it is important that we start on the same page with respect to the spiritual aspects of money and finances.

When we were children, the word "mine" was prevalent in our vocabulary, and we were told to share. In my own life, as I grew older and developed a personal relationship with God, I began to realize that God was actually sharing with me and giving me specific responsibilities for the things that he has put into my care. The more I understood that concept, the easier that it was for me to manage money because I grasped the true meaning of being a faithful steward of God's resources rather than exercise my selfish rights of ownership. The more I learned about stewardship the more my heart changed, and then my practices began to change as well.

One experience in my life stands out as a clear illustration of this perspective. As a new pastor, I remember pulling into a parking lot with a group of our youth in my car. Someone in the vehicle next to me hit my car door and the kids wanted to "go get him." My response to them was that "this is God's car. Let Him go get them if He wants." For me, it was just an off-handed remark, and I thought nothing more of the incident. Had I viewed it as "My car" then I would likely have had a very emotional response to the episode and been the first out of the car to "go get him."

Years later, some of those same kids returned to the church after they were grown and told me that they never forgot what I had said. It had become an example to them of the attitude of a steward – these are God's things, this is God's money, so if He wants to have an attitude about it, then I will receive His instruction. Otherwise, I don't need to be worried or emotional about it.

What is a Steward?

When the Bible speaks of a steward, it is talking in essence about a trustee — a person who manages and cares for the assets/property of another. The steward represents the owner as a caretaker, custodian, or chosen servant. 1 Corinthians 4:2 tells us that "…it is required that those who have been given a trust must prove faithful." Every believer is a steward because God has given each of us time, talents, and treasures to manage on His behalf, and use them to serve Christ. However, we can choose to manage the time, talents and treasures given us by God and become either a faithful or unfaithful steward. And according to scripture, financial freedom is only achieved by being a faithful steward.

As you can clearly see, it is impossible to be an owner and a steward at the same time. Stewards are responsible whether they are given little or much. With bigger blessings comes added responsibility. (Luke 12:48) The Lord expects that we will do a good job. When we put our trust in Him, He shows us His will and provides us the wisdom and strength to do His work. We become effective stewards when we live our lives in partnership with Christ. All of the promises God has made regarding His blessings in the area of finances are based on the idea that we surrender ownership. If we refuse to do this, we can never experience God's plan for our finances.

Understanding and mastering the interrelationship of the financial topics that we will explore —how they overlap and how they are used in God's plan for our lives — is paramount to achieving true financial freedom. God equates our ability to handle spiritual matters with our ability to manage our finances, and He uses money to help us learn obedience and to release His blessing in our lives.

Remember, the freedom that God wants to give you and me cannot be experienced in the area of finances unless we acknowledge God's ownership over everything and accept the role of a steward. It is up to God to decide whether or not to entrust us with wealth.

Purposes for Money

The world views money as a means for exercising power, control, security, independence, or influence. It is easy for Christians to get caught up into this perspective of money as well. God knew that finances would be a major issue throughout each era of history, and so gives us specific guidance through His Word. Scripture outlines the real purpose of money to accomplish the following:

- Provide basic needs — Philippians 4:19
- Confirm direction — Jeremiah 10:23
- Bless others — Romans 12:13
- Reveal God's power — 2 Corinthians 9:11
- Support the communication of the Gospel — 2 Corinthians 8 & 9

2 Corinthians 9:8 says, "And God is able to make all grace abound to you, that always having all sufficiency in everything, you may have an abun-

dance for every good deed."

God can also use money to help us learn obedience and to release His blessing in our lives. In his book, *Generous Living*, Ron Blue gives an insightful definition of money as tool, a test, and a testimony.

> "Money is a tool: We are not to hoard it, serve it, or pursue it as anything other than a means to an end. Since everything comes from God, and ultimately belongs to God, every decision we make — from giving to missions to buying a new pair of Nikes - has spiritual implications. Therefore we must ask the question, "Am I using my money the way God wants me to?"
>
> Money is a test: Money may serve as a test — financially, practically, and spiritually. The writer of Proverbs understood this when he said, "Give me neither poverty nor riches, but give me only my daily bread. Otherwise I may have too much and disown you and say, 'Who is the Lord?' Or I may become poor and steal, and so dishonor the name of my God." (Proverbs 30:8-9)
>
> Money is a testimony: How you use your money is a direct reflection of what you believe. If you truly believe that everything comes from God, you will use your money to accomplish His purposes, and that will stand as a testimony to the world. We pay a great price if we allow materialism to erode our testimony." [1]

Attitudes Toward Money

Our attitude toward money goes a long way toward revealing our heart for the things of God and our responsibility (and opportunity) to be a steward. The parable of the Good Samaritan (Luke 10:25-37) portrays three attitudes regarding stewardship through the characters:

- Attitude of the Robbers: What's yours is mine, and I'm going to take it.

- Attitude of the Priest & Levite: What's mine is mine, and I'm going to keep it.

- Attitude of the Samaritan: What's mine is yours, and I'm going to give it.

This last attitude is clearly the correct attitude for us to carry. God wants us to take the time to demonstrate with others the love He's shown us.

---

[1] Generous Living, by Ron Blue, Zondervan Publishing House, 1997, pages 57-59

Transferring Control to God

A humorous story is told of a man, hanging from a cliff a thousand feet above the ground. He was frightened and screamed, "Is there anyone up there who can help me?" Just then, he heard a booming voice from above that said, "Yes, I will help you. I am the Lord. Just relax and let go." There was a long pause. Then the man said, "Is there anyone else up there who can help me?"

Letting go is never easy, and relying on our own devices is a hard habit to break. It is challenging to release ourselves from our emotional attachments to material things so that we can use our God-given resources for His service. Transferring control is a faith issue that we wrestle with daily. Our goal is to learn how to give all we have to the Lord and trust Him to give back all we need.

God's Perspective On Money

Money is one of God's gifts and a very important part of our lives. However, many Christians lack a proper understanding of its purpose, and how to manage it. Our checkbooks tell us more about our values and priorities than just about anything else. That's why Jesus talked so much about money in the Bible. Sixteen of the 38 parables are concerned with how to handle money and possessions. Scripture offers 500 verses on prayer, fewer than 500 verses on faith, but more than 2,350 verses on money and possessions. The Lord knew that managing money and possessions was going to be a challenge for many people, so He wants us to know His perspective on this critical area of life.

Our society pressures us into focusing on defining our status and self worth through materialism. This pressure has caused many Christians to put God in a secondary position. God gives us the freedom to determine how we want to spend money, but the Bible is very clear about what God expects from us. The fact that God put all things, including money, at our disposal means that we are obligated to use them according to His plan to be wise stewards of all of life.

I have been struck by the vast number of Christians who are bound by financial issues. The pressure on their relationships, their inability to enjoy the present, and the frustration at not being able to support God's work is evident.

While the Apostle Paul encouraged us to learn to be content in any circumstance (Phil. 4:11) he did not suggest that we "park" at any place. We see from Paul's life that we should not accept any situation that limits us in serving the Lord. So, I have tried to write a practical book to share principles and action steps that will help you achieve financial freedom.

If you are burdened by debt and financial pressure, you don't have to stay there. You have the God-given power of decision. You can set your course to financial freedom. This book is a tool to assist you to put feet to that decision.

We live in a world of the "quick fix" and, as Christians, we sometimes look for something to "quickly fix" our financial situation. Unfortunately, we often end up in more trouble than when we started. God's ways are timeless, tried and true, and still apply today — even in this sophisticated world of on-line banking, Internet shopping, overnight millionaires, and global communication. God's ways are still "modern."

God is very present in our daily lives and has a plan for us to follow such a simple plan that is often missed, put aside until a later time, or overlooked altogether. It is up to us to acknowledge and respond to His directives.

Managing your finances is key to having a successful and fruitful Christian life. We must be free in our finances so that we can be responsive and faithful to God's directives. As I seek to live out my relationship with God, I have found that joy is not found just in having all my needs met, but in finding my needs met by God.

The Goal Of This Book

The purpose of this book is to help you experience the joy, peace, fulfillment, and contentment as a result of managing your God-given resources as a faithful steward. This book's content is based upon biblical stewardship principles. If you want to learn what God has to say about this area of your life, and recognize His authority over your life and the possessions He has entrusted to you as a steward, then you will benefit from this book.

How to Use This Book

As you read, I encourage you to stop and look up the scripture passages you find along the way. At the end of each chapter is an application section where you will find worksheets, places for actions and notes, and additional scriptures. I encourage you to work through these application sections and to open your Bible and learn God's Word for yourself.

Throughout this book you will be encouraged (or challenged) to evaluate your current beliefs, attitudes, and practices on a wide variety of financial topics. At the end of each chapter you will find a "For Application" section complete with checklists, worksheets, and other helpful tools.

Each chapter also includes a "Personal Finance Improvement Checklist," which will provide a list of action steps and/or reminders summarizing the chapter. I encourage you to carefully look them over and consider the ones that you need to put into practice. Prioritize these from the highest to the lowest priority, and then compare the actions that you check off with the goals that you will establish in the process of reading this book.

Learning to manage your finances is a journey that will take patience, planning and the ongoing re-commitment to do what God wants, no matter what everyone else is doing. It is tempting to think that an abundance of money will solve every problem. But many people who have much wealth, while achieving financial independence, do not experience financial freedom. They become slaves to their possessions. Only when we transfer control of our lives and our finances to God can we experience real financial freedom. I am hopeful that this book's unique combination of scriptural principles, practical worksheets, and reflective opportunities will help you achieve true financial freedom.

Freedom or Bondage

*When we are rightly focused,
we will trust in and delight ourselves
in the Lord and His Word,
and be balanced financially.*

Perhaps you know someone like my friend Mark. He received his MBA from one of the leading colleges in the U.S, began his career as a financial advisor for a top-notch company and was paid a salary well above the average for his age and experience. He had a wealth of financial planning tools at his disposal, all of which he used effectively. During this time in his life, his career, his financial plan and his new marriage were completely his to control. He was successful by all of the world's standards.

Mark became a Christian during junior high years, was involved with Campus Crusade for Christ on his college campus, and through CCC seminars, was given teaching on tithing and giving. But he had never asked God to take control of his finances.

Soon after their marriage Mark and his wife Jan purchased a nice home. Of course they wanted to furnish it and although they had a budget, it wasn't long before they had used all of their available credit and could barely make the required minimum payments while continuing to pay regular monthly bills. Although their home was new and nicely furnished there were still things they felt they "needed." Sometimes when they would talk about these "needs" Mark would feel uncomfortable and think, "Why is it that the more we have the more we want?"

Because of his financial background, Mark was invited to join the

NOTES

stewardship team at their church. He began to hear about opportunities to invest in the ministry of the local church and of missionaries. While he considered himself financially astute, all he could think of was, "I feel bound...if we just had more money I could give to the Lord's work." Think of it! Financially "successful" and still in financial bondage, loaded down with debt, nothing available to give, a feeling of growing discontent instead of satisfaction.

Mark and Jan are not alone. Three generations ago large personal debt was the exception not the rule. Your grandparents' philosophy, for the most part, was that if they didn't have the cash, they didn't buy the goods. This was the generation that went through the Depression and knew what it was like to do without.

The generation that followed modified that maxim somewhat. After World War II people wanted to buy homes, cars, and other big-ticket items and were willing to borrow for those items. Still, they were conservative when it came to short-term high interest debt, and they were more diligent about having a savings account. Yet, as the Baby Boomers progressed into mid-life, they became more and more comfortable with carrying multiple credit cards. Many pay them off each month, but an increasing number carry some high-interest debt, and even more of them have taken out second mortgages on their homes to finance their life-styles.

For today's generation, grandma & grandpa's frugal ideas have disappeared completely. For "Generation X" (now in their twenties and thirties), debt has become a way of life. They are the product of one of the longest economic booms in American history. During this time American consumers have piled up over $7.3 trillion in high-interest, short-term credit-card debt.

To put this in perspective, in 1952 consumer debt totaled a few million

NOTES

dollars. By 1980 that figure had gone up to about $2 trillion. Today it is nearly $8 trillion, which is an average of over $8 thousand per household! This is not debt for first mortgages on homes; this is credit-card debt! And many have used the increased valuation of their home as a piggy bank to live large. In the first half of 2001 American households borrowed a whopping $52 billion dollars by either refinancing their home or taking out a home equity loan (2nd mortgage). At the same time the average savings account, which was about 10% of the annual household income in 1975, has now dropped to an average of less than 1%. In 1980 we spent about 12% of our annual income on embellishments, wants, and luxury items. That figure has now risen to 20%.[1]

How can this happen you ask? This happens when, out of ignorance or disobedience, we fail to follow God's plan. Our money and what it will buy becomes our focus, and we find our security in financial assets rather than in the Lord. To fully understand God's plan for our financial freedom we must first take a close look at the many faces of " financial bondage."

Webster's Dictionary defines bondage as being controlled by someone or something, enslaved, having limited options or owned by someone or something.

A quick look around in your neighborhood, in your church, at the homes your friends and family have and the vehicles they drive can give you the impression that everything is profitable and prosperous. I wonder how many Mark and Jans are out there, looking successful and in control but actually in financial bondage and wishing for a way out.

Financial bondage may first rear its ugly head as we spiral downward into credit card /consumer debt. But the root cause is linked to two factors:

---

[1] Newsweek Magazine, August 27, 2001 issue, article title "Maxed Out!" by Daniel McGuinn, pages 34-39

NOTES

---

1) dissatisfaction with one's lot in life that drives us to lust for more, bigger and better; and 2) an incomplete knowledge of God's Word on finances and money. At this point we may simply think having more money or a larger credit line will solve the problem. This couldn't be further from what God has in mind.

Scripture makes it clear that having excessive debt is the greatest form of bondage. If a man who owed could not repay his obligations, then his lender had the right to put him in prison until he repaid every dollar. At that point everything that once belonged to the debtor – his family and all his possessions – now belonged to the lender.

There are several symptoms of bondage. Being able to recognize and detect these symptoms is an important first step in the process toward financial recovery:

- Overdue bills
- Investment worries
- "Get-rich-quick" attitude
- Deceitfulness
- Greed and covetousness
- Unmet family needs
- Work-aholism
- Money entanglements
- Financial unfairness
- Financial superiority
- Lack of commitment to God's work
- Focus on things rather than people

Take the quiz at the end of the chapter to help determine how much "financial bondage" you may be under. No matter where you land on this spectrum, there is hope for those who will put their trust in God. Even those who have financial security have a void if they fail to trust God.

Why do People Accumulate Wealth?
There are many reasons for why people accumulate wealth, which according to Scripture cause bondage. The reasons listed on the following page can be rectified through application of the truth found in Scripture.

NOTES

Reason	*Scripture's Response*
• Because others advise them to do it.	Seek God's wisdom before acting. (Prov. 15:22, Eph. 4:14)
• To "keep up with the Joneses" (envy).	Be on guard against greed and envy. (Ps. 73:2-3, Lk. 12:15)
• To provide security.	Put your hope in God, not in wealth. (1 Tim. 6:17, Rev. 3:17)
• For the love of money.	Keep your life free from this. (1 Tim. 6:10, Heb. 13:5)

These are not healthy or wise reasons to seek or accumulate wealth. However, Scripture does not say that accumulating wealth is wrong. God does not judge us by how much we have, but by our motivation, our attitude, and our actions regarding the accumulation of wealth. In fact, Scripture says that with wealth people can exercise their spiritual gifts and the grace of giving. (Rom 12:8, 2 Cor. 9:11, 2 Cor. 8:7, 1 Tim. 6:17-18)

Freedom or Fear

Fred and Alice's story illustrates that financial bondage can occur, not only by a lack of money or by overspending, but also from an abundance of money or misunderstanding why God gave it to us.

Fred and Alice worked hard all the years since they married. They were taught by their conservative, hard-working parents to save and to plan for a "rainy day." Fred devised a plan that would put them in their first home and eventually allow them to own one free and clear before many years passed. Fred

NOTES

learned the construction business from his Dad. Even though he was not skilled in all of the trades, he had friends willing to trade work skills with him. Using his knowledge of construction and his network of business contacts, he built their first home. Fred and Alice moved into their home, began making payments and saving to buy a lot for building another house. This got their plan going. From each home built and sold they made a profit, which went into the next home built and so on until they owned a home free and clear of debt.

While all of this was going on, Fred built his business from almost nothing to an organization with 35 employees and a net worth of close to $4 million dollars. Fred retired in his late 30's. Fred and Alice had it all. They loved the Lord, had financial security, and they could live the rest of their lives in comfort without having to work. This could be a story with a very happy ending, except for one missing ingredient.

Fred and Alice had stopped trusting God somewhere along the way and started trusting in their own efforts and wealth. Instead of being able to enjoy the security they had worked so hard to have, this wonderful couple lived in fear. Fear of losing their wealth, fear of having it taken from them, fear of having people in the leadership of their church discover they were wealthy and begin asking them for money. They feared that their money would not last as they grew older, and that they would find themselves dependent upon their children. Their hearts were filled with fear and their minds with questions. Would people like them for who they are or for what they have? Could they find a church home where they could worship without feeling that they needed to respond to every financial need? Fred and Alice succumbed to all of their fears. They isolated themselves, began living like hermits completely cut off from church, family and friends. Their world became the inside of their house.

NOTES

While it is wonderful to be debt free, God's plan is that all those who call themselves Christians live lives content in Him. We are to be comforted by the knowledge that our security is not in what we can earn, or what we have, or what we accomplish, but rather in God our Father who promises to meet all of our needs according to his glorious riches in Christ Jesus. (Phil. 4:19)

What is Financial Freedom?

Whether in wealth or in want, God's plan is for His people to understand and apply the following principles, which will lead to a life of contentment in Him and a life free from financial bondage.

1. Freedom from loving money and striving for more. Have you ever been caught in the trap of putting so much focus on money and possessions that your thoughts are on things rather than on God and His Word? I have. God says that the love of money is a root of all kinds of evil. (I Tim. 6:10) How can we apply this admonition to our daily lives, stay in balance and be sure to keep our "love" and need for money in right perspective? I Timothy 6:8 gives us a clue telling us that *"If we have food and clothing, we will be content with that."* Scripture then further challenges us to be content whether we enjoy abundance or suffer need. Knowing God's Word on this subject will help us keep a balance when the whole world is screaming, " If you just had more money all of your problems would be over."

"I have learned the secret of being content in every situation... whether living in plenty or in want" Phil. 4:12

When we strive for financial gain as a primary focus, we risk losing what I Tim. 6:6-8 calls *"godliness with contentment."* The Apostle Paul, while writing

---

NOTES

to Timothy used a term popular in Stoic philosophy, "contentment." The Stoic philosophy held that indifference or an impassive position on any issue was the way to have contentment. Self-sufficiency was the core of their belief system. Paul put it in Christian context, challenging all readers to trust God in all areas of their life and to be content to follow His plan and purpose. Paul says contentment is a feeling that comes from finding sufficiency in Christ. Godliness yields peace of mind and frees us from the stress produced when "things and money" control us. Contentment is both the sign of being truly God-centered and the reward of true godliness.

Beware! Don't be greedy for what you don't have.

Luke 12:15 NKJV

Is it always wrong to desire and strive for money? Not always. One can desire money for Christ-centered, not self-centered purposes. Paul assumes some will be rich (I Tim. 6:17-18). His counsel to the rich and all of us who want to honor God with our money is to be humble, to trust in God rather than money, and to be interested in good deeds, not bank accounts. The key is to focus on the right things. You cannot be financially free and in love with the "almighty dollar." It simply doesn't work that way.

Our culture's obsession to produce more leads to an obsession to acquire more. In the process, it leaves many of us feeling discontented with who we are and what we have. If we are stay-at-home parents, we feel left out of life. If we have a used automobile, we look toward having a brand new automobile. We want more, we want better, and we take pride in the wanting. It is an affliction of our times.[2]

---

[2] Seven Habits of a Healthy Home, by William Carmichael, VMI Publishers, Sisters, OR 2002, pg. 26

NOTES

2. Freedom from financial pressure. Have you ever found yourself with more month than money? Most of us have at some time been faced with that most unhappy circumstance. Financial pressure often occurs when we have not made provision for unexpected expenses or when we have lived beyond our means for a period of time. Those who study marriage and the family tell us that financial pressure is one of the key issues causing marriage relationships to break down and, if not resolved, too often leads to divorce. We will all encounter unexpected emergencies that will have financial ramifications. Making proper preparation will reduce the pressure.

In my experience, following a budget and saving for future needs (known and unknown) have been key practices in keeping my family from financial pressure. While most of us may not be able to have a large reserve developed, keep in mind that any savings is good. It will help cushion us in times of unexpected financial downturn.

The financial responsibility associated with life and the ensuing pressure or pleasure produced can be compared to the process occurring when we breathe. Healthy breathing causes our lungs to expand and contract supplying much needed oxygen. Our budget and/or financial plan must allow for the processes of life, which have increased and decreased financial need. When we allow these areas to become out of balance we live with fear and anxiety that allows the unexpected to create pressure and frustration.

3. Freedom from debt. One day, while I was serving as a pastor of a church, I received a call from Sally. She was absolutely desperate. Being a single parent with two children she had fallen into the habit of using a credit card to buy groceries and pay her utility bill. Sally often ran out of cash before the month was

NOTES

half over. When Sally called me she was facing her worst nightmare: a sick child, no health insurance, repairs needed on her car (her only transportation to work), and no available cash or credit. As her pastor I was thankful Sally felt she could call me, and I immediately felt the church should respond to this real need, which we did. The church wrapped their arms around Sally providing groceries to fill her cupboards, money to pay for the car repairs and providing gasoline and daily needs until her next payday. Someone stayed with her sick child so she could go to work and helped with medical bills until they had insurance. The church family stayed in touch, offering on-going assistance with budgeting and classes on personal finances until Sally and her family were out of debt and able to use credit appropriately. Sally now feels secure in her church family and is learning God's principles of financial stewardship.

"Let no debt remain outstanding…"
Rom. 13:8

"The rich rule over the poor, and the borrower is servant to the lender."
Prov. 22: 7

Anyone who has had past-due bills knows what it feels like to dread the inevitable collection call, demand note, payment deadline or unexpected crisis. When we are in debt we limit our options, lose flexibility, and are not able to adjust to meet short-term cash flow shortages, reductions in overtime pay, etc. In addition, we forfeit significant essentials to a happy productive life: contentment, security, peace of mind and the ability to give and contribute as God leads us. If you are struggling with overwhelming debt, a good financial plan with a regular system for saving and careful use of credit will help keep you free from bondage to debt.

4. Freedom from fear and worry over material needs and protection from compromise. When we are in debt, pressured and worried over our material

NOTES

needs, we give Satan a foothold. *"Therefore I tell you, do not worry about your life, what you will eat or drink, or what you will wear.... But seek first His Kingdom and His righteousness and all these things will be given to you as well."* (Matt. 6:25,33) Generally speaking most Christians do not plan to enter into unfair business practices; however, because of the fear that their material needs will not be adequately met, they are tempted to compromise honesty for gain. Excessive wealth or serious poverty can cause pressure, and lead to fear and worry. This kind of pressure can move people toward actions that are unethical and which would not normally be their modus operandi.

When the pursuit of money and the building of assets becomes our primary focus, we become men and women of the dollar rather than individuals who understand and live out the Lordship of Christ. Having a self-centered focus we can become involved (entangled) in unwise business dealings or fall prey to "get-rich-quick" schemes. When we are rightly focused, we will trust in and delight ourselves in the Lord and His Word and be balanced financially. This kind of balance prepares us to live ethically and with integrity. (James 5:1-4; Acts 24:16; I Peter 5:7; Phil. 4:6)

5. Freedom from "get-rich-quick" schemes. There are a million "opportunities" promising tremendous amounts of money with minimal, if any, effort. "Magic" results are promised without the work that those benefits would normally require. The Bible teaches that honest labor yields reward and that we are to "beware of ill-gotten gain." God's plan for the use of our time included work from the beginning. He gave clear instruction to Adam in the Garden of Eden: a regular schedule filled with tasks and daily communication with God the Father. Acquiring large amounts of money without the appropriate investment of

---

NOTES

ourselves is not God's plan. "Get-rich-quick" schemes are rooted in greed and can lead to putting sound financial principles aside and pursuing what we think will meet all of our needs at the expense of our relationship with the Lord and our families. "Get-rich-quick" schemes can turn a normal hope for security and provision into an insatiable desire for wealth. They can also be a financial disaster because they rarely deliver what they promise.

If you are not experiencing freedom in each of these five areas, then by definition you are caught in some degree of financial bondage. The good news is that, no matter how deep you've gotten yourself into financial quicksand, God has provided a way out. You can make some important decisions today that will positively affect your financial future, and put you on the road to recovery. Then, with time and discipline, you can learn to manage, as a wise and faithful steward, the financial resources that God has placed in your hands.

Why is Financial Freedom Important?

"If you have not been trustworthy in handling worldly wealth, who will trust you with true riches?" (Luke 16:11) God associates a person's ability to handle spiritual matters with his or her ability to handle financial matters. Financial freedom is key when the goal is to further God's work in this world.

- Financial freedom reduces worry and fear about the future. It is a step toward peace of mind.
- Financial freedom prepares God's people to give as He prompts.
- Financial freedom gained through obedience to God and his principles protects us from "get-rich-quick" schemes.

NOTES

Teaching Children about Financial Freedom

One the best gifts that we can give to our children, after accepting Christ as their personal Savior, is the proper handling and attitudes toward money. This is a foundation of teaching that we can begin when they are young, so that when they are grown they will have skills to be financially free and know how to honor God with their finances. Parents and grandparents bear the primary responsibility of teaching children about wise stewardship and financial principles and attitudes. Children learn from a combination of direct instruction, observation, and hands-on activity. Furthermore, parents should recognize that teaching attitudes about money is just as important — if not more so — as teaching them the mechanics of writing a budget and managing a checkbook.

"Now to him who is able to do immeasurably more than all we ask or imagine, according to his power that is at work in us."

Eph. 3:20

The key is to begin as early as possible with your children, taking advantage of teaching opportunities as they present themselves. Throughout this book there will be brief discussions about how to teach children about goals and budgeting, saving, debt, and giving. These are designed to help you focus on giving children a good financial foundation before they strike out on their own. I am motivated by this subject in part because I recently heard a shocking statistic that the average college undergraduate has $1,834 in credit card debt and nine percent have card debt between $3,000 and $7,000. This speaks to the need today to teach our children that the culture of debt may seem normal, but it is not healthy.

NOTES

Taking Practical Steps Toward Financial Freedom

Understanding how financial principles are used in God's overall plan for our lives is the first step toward financial freedom. This could be a frightening thought unless we understand that God wants to teach and train us, using money as a tool, to help us learn obedience, and to release His blessing in our lives.

In the next chapters we will look at some financial concepts and how understanding and practicing basic biblical principles will release the power of God in our lives like nothing we have ever experienced.

NOTES

For Application

Following is a quiz to help you determine if you may be in financial bondage.

Quiz: Am I in Financial Bondage?	(Circle One)
1. I have more than one credit card.	True False
2. I have more than three credit cards.	True False
3. I carry a balance on my credit card(s) and pay interest.	True False
4. I have bounced a personal check more than once this past year.	True False
5. I often can only pay the minimum on monthly bills.	True False
6. I sometimes buy more than what is on my list when I go shopping.	True False
7. When I see something I want "On Sale," it is hard for me to resist purchasing it even if I had not planned to buy it before going shopping.	True False
8. I love to shop. I feel good while shopping.	True False
9. I have had to borrow money from friends or relatives this past year.	True False
10. If I had to replace a transmission or a water heater tomorrow, I would need to borrow the money.	True False
11. I think about money a lot and feel some stress that I don't have more.	True False
12. I have received a collection letter or a phone call from a collection agency in the past year for past due bills.	True False
13. I regularly use the ATM machines to withdraw the cash I need.	True False
14. I rarely use my bank statement to reconcile or balance my checkbook.	True False
15. I am maxed out on one or more credit cards.	True False
16. I have been unable to give to a charity or my church this month.	True False
17. I have used my credit card this past year for discretionary items such as new clothes, CD's, vacations, eating out, etc., even though I carry a balance.	True False

18. I do not have, or make regular contributions to an IRA or savings account.	True	False
19. I do not have a written down monthly spending budget.	True	False
20. My job does not pay me enough.	True	False

How to Score: For every "true" answer, give yourself one point.

Score of 0-5. Okay to Excellent: You have most financial matters under control. You probably have a savings account. Most likely, if you have a credit card, you pay it off every month. You no doubt have a budget and a good fix on the future. For the most part, you are able to resist the temptation to impulse buy and you give regularly to your church. But beware of some "bondage" problems if you scored a 4 or 5.

Score of 6-10. Borderline to On the Edge. You no doubt know you have some spending/budget problems, and while you are making it okay right now, you know that if circumstances were to change you could go over the edge and be in financial trouble. You do feel financial bondage. You and your spouse are working hard each month just to keep your heads above water. The future for you is tentative, and you have much more debt that you should. You are either considering a refinance/home equity loan or you have already made one. You need to take some serious steps to improve your situation.

Score of 11 to 15. Big Trouble to Drowning. For some of you, your big problems are more recent since an unplanned crisis came along that devastated your finances. Most people with these scores are delinquent and are barely keeping the "wolves from the door." You are borrowed up to the max without knowing how you will pay it back. You are still thinking about how to pay back what you owe or how to consolidate debt to free up yet another credit card balance. You have not given much thought to how to cut back spending. You need to get credit/financial counseling right away.

Score of 16 or more. The other "B" word is tempting you. "Bondage" has forced you to think of the other "B" word...."Bankruptcy." You have no doubt given it serious consideration or have filed already. Your credit is ruined and collection calls and threats are a regular thing for you. Repossession of cars or property is eminent if not already happening. Credit cards and checking accounts are non-existent for you since most of you have already lost those privileges.

Following is a quiz to help you determine if you may be vulnerable to "Get-Rich-Quick" schemes.

Quiz: Are You Vulnerable to "Get-Rich-Quick" Schemes?　　(Circle One)

1. I have invested (time and/or money) in at least one multi-level marketing opportunity (MLM) in the past year.	True　False
2. Whenever I hear about a moneymaking opportunity that is almost too good to be true, I am strangely attracted to it.	True　False
3. I have bought lottery tickets more than once.	True　False
4. I buy lottery tickets frequently.	True　False
5. I have purchased stocks based on tips from friends who told me the stock was a "slam dunk."	True　False
6. I have invested in "opportunities" that sounded great and promised a big return that, at the time I invested, I didn't fully understand. Only later did I realize what was going on.	True　False
7. I believe a lot of wealth is generated by "being in the right place at the right time" rather than being generated through hard work.	True　False
8. While I am not proud of it now, I have borrowed money to invest in a scheme that later went sour.	True　False

Results: The more "true" answers you have, the more you are prone to make a mistake and fall for a "get-rich-quick" scheme that usually produces more heartache than wealth. You need to be sure to seek counsel from a trusted financial advisor before investing in anything.

Reflections on Freedom or Bondage

1. Take a moment to reflect on what you have just read and the quizzes you have taken. Be honest with yourself and with God. Are you under financial bondage? If so, ask God to help you and give you both wisdom and the willpower to overcome this bondage. Confess your need of help to God and ask Him for divine guidance.

2. **Read Matthew 6:19 and 24-35.** Jesus is talking about a basic core value that affects our ability to live in financial freedom – where do we put our trust and our life focus? Think about your personal attitudes and values about money and possessions. Where are your treasures stored, and which master do you serve today?

3. Our culture pressures us to have certain things and to look a certain way or we will be viewed as unsuccessful. This causes undue anxiety and stress about keeping up appearances. How do you deal with this pressure to conform? **Read I Peter 5:7, Philippians 4:6, and II Corinthians 10:12**

4. Regardless of your current financial position and future goals, it is possible to experience contentment if your focus is on God. **I Timothy 6:6-13** says that godliness with contentment is great gain, referring to the internal condition of the heart rather the external condition of circumstances. Lack of contentment is often the root of all kinds of financial issues. What is your heart condition today? Whether in wealth or in want, do you lack contentment? Describe ways that you may be expressing discontent through your spending habits.

    _____

    _____

5. Write down/journal your thoughts about financial freedom. _____

    _____

    _____

6. Additional scriptures for review and reflection:
    Matthew 13:22, Romans 12:1-3, James 5:1-4, Galatians 6:7-9, Ephesians 4:17-24

7. Now it's time to be brutally honest. If you (and/or your spouse) are in bondage over your attitudes about money, pray this prayer sincerely:

"Lord, I confess that I have not been trusting you to be my provider, and I have not been trusting you to be Lord over all that I have. I realize that my heart has been following after "things" and not looking to you. I ask you to forgive me and to help me make the necessary changes that will bring true freedom to my life. Amen."

NOTES

Receiving God's Provision

*"Seek first His Kingdom
and His Righteousness,
and all of the other things
will be given to you."
Matt. 6:33*

Shortly before my sixth birthday, my father died, leaving Mom and me alone and on a limited income. In spite of our circumstances, Mom believed that we should do our part to help anyone less fortunate than we were. Sometimes there were things I wanted and, when I would ask for something, Mom would say, "I'm sorry, we just can't afford that. God will provide what you need." One of Mom's favorite sayings was, "It is more blessed to give than to receive." (Acts 20:35) And give we did, often giving away something we could have used or money I thought could be used to purchase something I wanted. Being a literal child, sometimes I thought, "It is fun to give, but why does Mom work so hard and then just give away what she gets?" I had a lot to learn about what the Lord Jesus meant when He spoke the words, "It is better to give than to receive." Jesus was talking about the Lordship and stewardship of all we are and have. I was thinking about what I wanted, and what my friends had, and the difference between us.

How Do We Receive God's Provision?

In the Sermon on the Mount (Matt. 5-7), Jesus tells us not to worry about what we will eat or drink or about what we will wear because He promises to provide for our needs. Instead of worrying, He instructs us to *Seek first His Kingdom and His righteousness, and all of the other things will be given to us.*

NOTES

Have you ever wondered why Jesus even bothered to say that at this time? I would suppose that the people listening to Jesus that day must have been worrying about some of the same things we worry about, and they came to Jesus with their worries. When this passage was written, Jesus' followers had daily lives just as we do. He was asking them to follow Him, put Him first, and to put the work of His Kingdom before their own needs and wants.

Being a man with a family, I think I know how they were feeling. Sometimes I wonder if I can provide all that is needed to feed, clothe and give my family a good life. How often have you heard someone

"Lazy hands make a man poor, but diligent hands bring wealth."

Prov. 10:4

say, "Don't worry, God will provide?" Have you ever been in a tight situation, needing money or help, and had a fellow Christian say that to you? How did it feel? Did you wonder how the Lord would provide? If you are in the business of making things happen and providing all of your own needs, don't be surprised if being told "not to worry, God will provide" makes you feel a bit angry. Sometimes I have thought, "How does this apply to my life? I work hard for what I have and what I give my family. Does God use my work to provide? I know God wants me to work. Am I trusting Him to provide when I work, save, plan and pray?" What is the balance between my work and God's provision? They are in truth the same.

In fact, Scripture addresses our responsibility to faithfully provide for our families and ourselves through work. The parable of the ambitious ant in Proverbs 6:6-11 tells us that if we are slack and do not earn our way, poverty will come upon our families and us. This same admonition about work is found in 1 Timothy 5:8, *"But if anyone does not provide for his relatives, and especially*

NOTES

for his immediate family, he has denied the faith and is worse than an unbeliever."

Jesus' Words

Let's take another look at Jesus' words in the Sermon on the Mount. The key words are, *"Seek first His Kingdom and His righteousness, and all of the other things will be given to us."* What are His Kingdom and His Righteousness? His Kingdom is all of heaven and earth — the now and the not yet. His righteousness is the gift we are given when we receive Christ as Savior and Lord and live our lives as He wants.

As an adult I can still hear my mother's voice as she said, "It is more blessed to give than to receive." When I questioned her, she would say that when we put God first with our money, and in our lives we will receive His provision for us. Mom believed God provided her a job. She worked hard, gave faithfully, and trusted God to bless her efforts. My mother's example illustrates one of God's most significant avenues of provision for you and me–work.

Receiving God's Provision Through Work

Deuteronomy 8:18 encourages us to, *"Remember the Lord our God, for it is He who gives you the ability to produce wealth."* Greeks of Old Testament relegated physical work to slaves and other inferiors, later learning that the God of the Jews actually worked. What a strange God – with power to create the world in six days and only choosing to take one day of rest. (Gen. 2:2) The fact that God worked at all teaches us its value. The universe expresses what the work done by the hand of a powerful God can accomplish. If the work of creation is an expression of God's being, can't we also assume that man's work expresses our being–especially since we are created in God's image and we are expected to be parallel to His being?

NOTES

What's So Important About Work?

"The Lord God took the man and put him in the Garden of Eden to work it and take care of it." (Gen. 2:15) As Adam played out his role, he took his designated place in the interrelated plan of creation. There was a specific place for him in the garden. It was his task to keep order and balance in Eden. He worked.

Adam experienced the significance of his own being through acting and working effectively. What a delight it must have been for Adam to cultivate the ground for the express pleasure of God! Their relationship was such that God's pleasure was Adam's pleasure and their pleasure came through work. Questions about meaning and purpose for life were absurd, in fact, they were inconceivable at that time.

"I was young and now I am old, yet I have never seen the righteous forsaken or their children begging for bread."

Psalm 37:25

Sin Made Work Hard

The events following man's and woman's choice to sin changed our relationship with God and all that had been created. The result of sin is not that we have to work, but that we have to work by the sweat of our brow. We often no longer see work as a pleasure and a pure expression of our being. Knowing we must work in order to provide for our own physical needs corrupts our outlook. We can become preoccupied with work and wages, and exist in a spiritual blindness that blocks the vision that Adam had in the garden. When you think about it, it would be a blessing in itself for contemporary Christians to capture the vision and knowledge that everything we do can be done for the glory of God, including work. We have been restored to fellowship with God through Christ. Our everyday work can become, at least to some degree, the equivalent of Adam's

NOTES

tilling the garden–a pleasure, a delight, a meaningful activity and the way God has provided for us to receive His provision.

God, as Lord of our lives, has provided work which gives us the money we need for daily needs, a means to contribute to our community and also a vehicle for building our skills and self-confidence. As we work and receive money in exchange for our time and contribution, God's plan also includes giving the first portion to Him (the tithe, which will be discussed later in this book), giving to special needs (offerings) as He leads, and also saving for future needs.

Receiving God's Provision Through Saving

Later, in chapter six, we will discuss in greater detail the principles, purposes and vehicles for saving. But at this point in our discussion, it is appropriate to acknowledge that saving is also a spiritual issue. In *The Word on Finances* by Larry Burkett, we read:

It is not unspiritual to save; nor does it represent a lack of faith. This is one principle that God's people need to learn and practice more. To put money into savings means you have the ability to store money for the purchase of a future need. Too often we use credit–the reverse of savings. When you use credit you buy a product, then try to pay the purchase price later. Unfortunately, the price also incurs an interest charge, which makes that payment even more difficult.

A far better concept taught in God's Word is to sacrifice in the short-term to attain long-term goals. It is important to budget some savings. Otherwise, the use of credit becomes a lifelong necessity and debt a way of life. Savings allow you to purchase with cash and shop for the best buys.[3]

NOTES

Begin a savings fund. No matter how small, no matter how inadequate, a beginning is a beginning. The key is to start, even as little as $5 or $10 per paycheck. It will add up! When you choose to save, you are receiving God's provision. When you have savings, God can use you and what He has provided for you to meet your needs and to bless others.

Early in our marriage my wife and I determined to obey God by choosing to tithe faithfully and, in addition, we tried to save regularly. When we were first in the pastorate, our salary was adequate but did not allow for emergencies or extra things we wanted or needed. One morning as I was showering before leaving for the church, the hot water suddenly turned cold. I thought, "No hot water...broken hot water heater...what will this cost?" I grabbed a towel, pulled on some shorts and went to the kitchen where Connie was making breakfast. Her response to our dilemma was, "You are the 'prophet and priest' of our home, go and lay hands on it and pray." Picture this. I am in the utility room in my shorts with my hands on the water heater, praying, "Lord please touch this water heater and make it work. You know we don't have enough saved to buy a new one." We waited 30 minutes and tried the water again. It was hot and stayed hot for nine months. When the water heater went out again we had saved $350 and were able to buy a new one. I believe God honored my prayer because we honored Him with our tithe. Then His provision came through our savings.

Receiving God's Provision Through Prayer

The term "provision" has evolved in our day. When our grandparents were young, God's provision meant "enough to get by." Provision does mean we

---

[3] The Word on Finances, by Larry Burkett, Moody Press, 1994, page 352

NOTES

will have enough to get by, but today we have gone far beyond that. Sometimes the availability of credit insulates our lives from the kind of needs that God desires to meet through prayer. The challenge is to be willing to look to God honestly, asking Him to help us separate our needs from our wants. When this is done, we can faithfully save, continuing to depend upon God to show us how to use the money we save. We can make the things we want to purchase a matter of prayer, asking God for direction. He will surprise us every time.

God's promise in Phil. 4:19, *"And my God will meet all your needs according to His glorious riches in Christ Jesus,"* has little relevance in a life where there are no needs; and often serves as a stumbling block to faith when applied to "wants." Wants could be biblically defined as "whims and desires." All of us have much to be thankful for when we consider the number of needs that God meets for us each day through work, savings, and His provision. Be encouraged by Luke 11:11–13, which says, *"Which of you fathers, if your son asks for a fish, will give him a snake instead? Or if he asks for an egg, will give him a scorpion? If you then, though you are evil, know how to give good gifts to your children, how much more will your Father in Heaven give the Holy Spirit to those who ask Him!"*

Teaching Children About God's Provision

It is critical to understand that children receive much of their instruction through observation and by example. When we give credit to God for His daily provision, we are teaching our children to recognize the source of all that we have. Once we acknowledge this fact, it is easy to see how important it is to reflect a heart of gratitude to God for our work, our shelter, our food, clothing, and the "extras" that we get to do and buy.

NOTES

One way to teach children about God's provision is to involve them in praying for your wants and needs. Then, when those prayers are answered, remind the kids that this is what you were praying to God about and thank Him for His answer. There will be opportunities for your children to do this with their own needs as well, and it will be helpful for you to identify these times and guide them through it.

Even as adults, when we think of God's provision, it is tempting to remember only those times when "God bailed us out." In the application section at the end of this chapter there is a Checklist of God's Provision designed to help you identify God's hand of provision in your daily life. Consider completing the "Checklist of God's Provision"with your children. As you fill in the blank spaces with your own thoughts of God's provision in your personal life, take notice of how many things that you identify go well beyond the basic needs of food, shelter, and clothing. Isn't our God good?

NOTES

For Application

Personal Finance Improvement Checklist

____ List your needs on a sheet of paper, then try to identify the "needs" that are actually "wants" or "desires." Analyze your attitude toward these categories. Do you need to make any adjustments to your list or your attitude?

____ Consider your work as a form of God's provision. How does this perspective change your outlook of your job or daily work? How can you see that God has a purpose for your job today?

A Checklist Of God's Provisions
Check the things that God has provided for you.

___Salvation

___The Bible

___ Health

___ A job

___ Family

___Shelter

___Basic food

___Clothing

___A car/transportation

___Friends

___A church

___Beauty in nature

___Educational opportunities

___Democracy

___Love

___A pet

___A mentor

___Electricity

___Modern plumbing

___Paved roads

___Policemen

___ Firemen

___ Ambulances & EMTs

___Modern medicine

___Extras: (favorite foods, work benefits, favorite hobby/recreation, special people, good fortune, miracles) List them below...

_____

_____

_____

_____

_____

_____

_____

Reflections on Receiving God's provision

1. Take a moment to reflect on the list of God's provision. Prayerfully thank Him for all of these provisions and ask Him to continue to give you a grateful heart for all of the good things He continually provides for you.

2. **Read Proverbs 3:11-18** – How does this passage reflect an aspect of God's provision for you? Do you see His discipline and correction as a way for Him to open your life to receive His blessings, both spiritually and materially? How has God provided for you through the gifts of wisdom and understanding?_____

   _____

   _____

3. **Read Genesis 2:15, Deuteronomy 8:17 – 19 and Proverbs 6:6-11**
   What do you think about the perspective of God's provision through work? Have you thought that it was by your own effort that you provide for yourself and your family? Do you have a different view of work now? If so, how?_____

   _____

   _____

4. Have you given the Lord opportunity to provide for your needs through prayer, or has your practice been to buy as you go? **Read Philippians 4:5-7** and ask God to help you remember to make your requests to Him and to wait for His provision.

5. Reflect on your reading of the chapter and identify the various ways that you have experienced God's provision. _____

   _____

   _____

6. Additional scriptures for review and reflection:
   Proverbs 10:3-5, 13:22, Mark 11:24

Prayer: *Lord, you are the Great Provider and you have faithfully provided for me through work, saving, and through prayer. I confess that that I have often taken matters into my own hands and have forgotten to make my requests known to you. Help me today to start a new discipline of talking to you about my needs and desires and waiting for your answer. Amen.*

CHAPTER 3

Budgeting

An accurate budget is your personal spending plan, which is based on a set of goals that you develop. This combination of goals and budget is a tool which can and will help provide all you need.

Janey grew up in an affluent family, able to have just about anything she desired at just about anytime she wanted it. During her college years her parents were in a position to assist her with school and living expenses. Janey had never thought about living on a budget. Tom, her new husband, had a very different upbringing. He was from a less affluent family. He learned at an early age that he had to work for what he wanted. He learned to budget in order to make the money he did have go for the purposes he intended. In order to attend college Tom had to hold down two, sometimes three, jobs. He learned to control his expenditures so that his school and living expenses could be met.

It's not hard to believe that they had very different ideas about the need for and function of a budget. Both Janey and Tom sometimes wondered why their budget caused friction between them. Budgeting dictated that they wait for things, confer with each other and follow a plan. This created friction because of the way they were raised. Perhaps you have experienced a similar problem.

Many people have a mistaken view that budgeting is intended to put restrictions on them until they have no financial freedom, so the issue of budgeting becomes repugnant to them. A budget is simply a road map that helps you advance toward goals that you have established. A budget doesn't tell you how to spend your money; you tell your budget how you choose to spend your money. The best way to determine how you will spend your money is to first set

---

NOTES

some clear financial goals. Remember that no one is going to give, save, or reduce debt for you. It's really up to you to make it happen.

Why Set Goals?

It is not very practical to discuss budgeting without first thinking about goal setting and actually working through the process of establishing financial goals. Goals are measurable objectives that you believe God wants you to achieve. And a budget is one tool to help you achieve those goals.

"Is there anyone here who, planning to build a new house, doesn't first sit down and figure the cost so you'll know if you can complete it?"
Luke 14:28 (The Message)

Our society is always on the run — but much of the time we're not sure where we're going. When we focus on the pressures of the day rather than setting goals for the future, we become like the man who was driving through the Cascade Mountains in a snowstorm. He lost all sense of direction until he saw a snow plow. Relieved, he kept as close to the vehicle as he could while it removed snow from the pavement. At times the heavy snowfall made it difficult to follow the plow. After a while, the plow stopped and the operator got out and walked over to the car. "Mister, where are you headed?" the driver asked. "I'm on my way to Montana." the man responded. "Well, you'll never get there following me. I'm plowing out this parking lot!"

Failing to Plan Can be Costly

Good planning helps us be alert to potential pitfalls, and allows us to fix things when they go bad rather than react to crisis situations. When you don't

NOTES

44

make a serious financial plan that you intend to follow, you could also be losing out on a lot of opportunities. Failing to plan could mean that you:

➤ May have to pay higher taxes than necessary.

➤ May not have enough money for education or retirement.

➤ May lack insurance protection from auto, home or work related accidents.

➤ May not reach your God-given goals and potential.

➤ May have to go into debt for auto and home repairs and other expenses.

There are a number of reasons why we don't plan.

➤ They lack the knowledge or ability to plan — there is a saying, "People don't plan to fail, they fail to plan."

➤ Planning forces us to consider unpleasant topics and events such as debt, unemployment, disability, and death.

➤ Planning places limits on us and makes us accountable.

➤ We may think we need expensive professional guidance.

➤ We feel we don't have enough assets or income to bother with planning.

The story of Joseph in Genesis chapters 37 through 47 offers some insight into the importance of planning. God gave Joseph the wisdom to plan and set goals, sparing Egypt from much suffering. God wants to give you the same ability in order to spare you and your family from potential suffering and hardship.

Guidelines for Setting Goals

1. A goal is a measurable and time-specific objective toward which you believe God wants you to move. It goes beyond "Wouldn't it be nice if..." or "I'd

---

NOTES

really like to have…"

2. Set your goals and standards on God's conviction — not on what others possess.
3. Goals need to be realistic, practical, reachable, and have deadlines.
4. Faith-sized goals that stretch you and require God's help should be considered.
5. Financial goals change as circumstances change, so be flexible and patient.
6. Goals need to be written down - creating more accountability and motivation.
7. Each goal needs a set of plans to reach it, with a beginning and completion date for each step along the way.
8. You may need the help of others in order to create plans and find tools to reach the goals.
9. Setting goals requires uninterrupted time, attention, and serious commitment.
10. Every goal needs to be prayerfully considered and have ownership by all parties involved in achieving the goal (such as a husband and wife and/or children).

Below is a list of some sample goal statements. Note how they clearly state the objective in dollars and also offer a clear deadline.

➤ Assist my two children with four years of college education at a cost of $20,000 each, beginning in two years and ten years.
➤ Save $25,000 by age 30; $75,000 by age 40; and $110,000 by age 45.
➤ Buy a $15,000 car for cash in three years.
➤ Pay off credit debt of $2,000 within two years.

Evaluating Your Goals

After you list your goals, and as you establish plans for reaching them,

---

NOTES

here are a few goal-setting questions to consider:

➤ What obstacles or problems might you encounter?

➤ What additional data do you need to collect or research?

➤ What additional training or skills do you need?

➤ What additional resources do you need?

➤ How much money will it take to meet your needs?

➤ Are there other ways to accomplish your goals? If so, list them.

➤ Do you need to create a back-up plan for any of your goals/plans?

➤ What are the spiritual and temporal benefits of accomplishing your goals?

➤ Are you keeping your goals visible so you stay on the right track?

Procrastination is one of the greatest hindrances to financial planning. But Galatians 6 reminds us that we reap what we sow. If you sow nothing (don't plan), you reap nothing. If you sow too late, you reap a limited harvest!

In the "For Application" section at the end of this chapter, you will find some helpful worksheets to assist in your goal development process. The points to remember are that any goals you set must be very specific, must have a plan for accomplishing the goal, and must have a deadline.

Teaching Children About Goals

It is easy to overlook the value of goal setting for children, especially when it can be so difficult for us to do as adults. However, helping children set achievable goals is a very practical and beneficial experience. It will encourage them to work toward achievements on their own, help them to develop a sense of initiative and personal responsibility, as well as teach them the discipline of delayed gratification. When parents or grandparents give their children or grand-

NOTES

children everything they ask for, they miss a great teaching opportunity. Providing for a child's basic needs is a natural parental response. But immediately fulfilling their "wants" (which they refer to as "needs") has many shortcomings. By doing so you take away their motivation to learn and practice ways for earning and saving money and setting goals, all of which will be invaluable life lessons. The discipline needed for a ten-year-old to save part of his or her allowance weekly and buy a new $100 bicycle over a one-year period, instead of squandering it on candy and pop, is the same discipline required of an adult to save $10,000 over three years to buy a newer car for cash rather than purchase it on credit. Everyone needs to learn the rewards of setting and attaining short and long-term financial goals, and to experience the satisfaction of personal achievement. And the sooner one can learn these lessons the better.

Budgeting to Achieve Your Goals

Now that we have discussed the importance and process for goal setting, we are ready to discuss the nuts and bolts of how to put a plan in place for achieving your financial goals. We will call this plan a "budget."

If you have goals to reduce your debt, to increase your savings, to plan for retirement, and to live contentedly and comfortably, it's essential that you have a financial plan that will lean heavily on a budget. Your plan needs to be flexible, but also to be a tool that will help you to control erratic spending habits. In a sense, you are choosing to treat your household like a business. As you execute a well-structured budget, you will achieve peace of mind and a firm grip on your financial future.

NOTES

Where to Start

A common question about goal setting and budgeting, is "Where do I start?" It's one thing to know that you have a lot of credit card payments or that funds are tight, but it's another thing to nail down some actual figures for a starting place. A good way to measure your current financial position is to calculate your net worth. This is a total of the value what you own (your assets) minus the total of what you owe (your liabilities). Improving your net worth is also a good measurement to use as you work your way through specific goals, such as increasing savings, paying off debt, purchasing a home, etc. Use the worksheet at the end of this chapter to determine your current net worth.

Budgeting vs. Record Keeping

An appropriate budget will include long-term and short-term savings. Just writing down every penny you spend is record keeping, not budgeting. Budgeting is prospective. It's financial planning that has been checked and evaluated by record keeping.

The components of a well-structured budget are determined wholly by the needs of the individual or family for whom it is devised. Basically, it is a list of income from all sources and a list of all expected expenses. Once all expenses are accounted for, they must be structured in such a way as to meet all of your goals and requirements.

Benefits of a Good Budget

Since a budget is simply a road map that you design to help you move toward your planned goals, the mystery and agony of budgeting does not need to exist any longer. There are a number of benefits to having a good budget that you

NOTES

should consider as you decide whether this is something that you really intend to do for yourself or not.

- A budget can help you see where your money is going, and it can help you decide where and how much you can spend.
- Budgeting can empower you to make intelligent and responsible decisions about the best possible use of your money and to live within your means.

Some people need to live on a strict paycheck-to-paycheck budget, while others don't require such a tight budget. But either way, a well-conceived budget will be flexible enough to allow for necessary adjustments, yet disciplined enough to control erratic spending habits.

70/20/10 – How to create a budget you can stick to.

The method described below is a sound financial tool to help you develop your budget. These percentages will give you a clear target to determine if you are on track or out of whack.

- Look at your anticipated gross income, and first calculate your 10% tithe on this year's gross income.
- Subtract that tithe as well as any financial gifts above your tithe that you have <u>committed</u> to pay, and come up with a subtotal.
- Reduce that subtotal by payroll deductions and payroll taxes. Payroll deductions may be a retirement program contribution, 401(k) or 403(b) contributions, hospitalization coverage, etc. Now you have arrived at your net take home pay. This figure becomes 100% of your usable income.

From this point forward there is a simple formula. Live on 70%, use no

NOTES

more than 20% for debt retirement and save 10% or more. Once you have eliminated debt, that 20% becomes discretionary and can be used for additional giving, additional savings or for other planned expenditures. You should note that your house payment comes out of the 70% and not out of the debt retirement portion. A worksheet is provided at the end of the chapter for your assistance in planning a budget.

Budget Maintenance

For your budget to run smoothly, you should take time to review and evaluate it. I recommend that each month you compare your budget with your actual expenditures and determine where you're overspending or underspending. Developing and maintaining a budget takes patience and practice. Remember it is okay to begin again. The key is to set aside time each month to review your budget—perhaps, at the same time that you balance your checking account. Look at your spending patterns to see if they're in line with your budget and in line with your financial plan.

Another option to maintaining your budget is the Cash Management Method. This is a practical system for those who have difficulty sticking to a budget when credit cards, debit cards and checks make funds so readily spendable. It is easy to set up and requires very little bookkeeping.

The Cash Management Method

Thousands of people have found the Cash Management Method to be the only effective way to curb overspending, to provide money for savings and investments, and to help determine how much cash they have available at all times. It means you reduce check writing and tracking, avoid bank overdraft

NOTES

charges, learn to limit credit card spending, and manage your finances so you can reach your financial stewardship goals.

Getting started with a Cash Management System

1. Divide 100% of your income to the following three areas:
   - Fixed Expenses - Tithe, mortgage, credit, insurance, utilities, taxes, etc. You receive a bill for these or they come on a steady basis. Only money to pay these expenses is to be put in your checking account.
   - Savings & Investments — Money for emergencies, short- and long-term goals, retirement, etc. Deposit these funds directly into your savings, investment, and retirement accounts.
   - Variable Expenses – Determine how you want to divide the rest of your income for other expenses, like groceries, entertainment, gifts, clothing, auto expense, etc. NOTE: Do not put this money into your checking account! Instead, place cash into envelopes marked for each expense/purchase category, and only use cash for these purchases. When an envelope is empty, you have depleted that area of your budget until your next pay period.

Guidelines and Flexibility

- If you have cash left in an envelope toward the end of the month (and cannot anticipate any more expenses in that area for the month), you may use it to pay a necessary expense in an area that no longer has funds available.
- If you underspend in one or more areas during the month, you can carry over any unused money to the next month, or place it in your "Miscellaneous" envelope.

NOTES

- Make envelopes for each expense listed on the "variable expenses" section of your "Current Income and Expense Worksheet" found in step four of the Application section at the end of this chapter.
- Keep current month expense receipts in marked envelopes in a safe place.
- Put a "Monthly Budget Account Sheet" (provided in the chapter) in each envelope and track the monthly balance.

Teaching Children about Budgeting

We can begin to teach our children about budgeting at an early age with a very practical hands-on technique that is described in Larry Burkett's book, *The World's Easiest Guide to Finances*. He suggests that parents set up three piggy banks (or money containers) in the child's room – one for giving (or tithes), one for savings, and one for spending. Then, any money that the child receives (through allowance, gifts, or odd-jobs) is to be divided into these containers. To make budgeting easier, give them their allowance money in change or small bills so that it is easy for them to see how much each bank should receive.   One suggestion is to allocate 10% to the tithe container, 50% to the savings container, and 40% to the spending container. Setting goals for the spending and the savings containers is a critical aspect of the teaching process. Children need to experience success, so when they reach their savings goals be sure to celebrate. As children mature and develop a better grasp of the financial aspects that you are teaching, you can direct them into managing their finances through a notebook or a check register and also identify a household bill or two that they can be responsible for. Teaching children how to handle finances early through budgeting equips them with a healthy perspective of the reality that money doesn't grow on trees and that it must be managed properly in order for

NOTES

us to be able to purchase those things that we need and want.

Practical Budgeting Tips

Many people struggle with budgeting and don't stick with it long enough to see how well it can work because they associate a budget with restriction. An accurate budget is your personal spending plan, a tool which can and will help you give according to your stewardship goals, provide all you need, and help you achieve many of the things you are dreaming of having. The following tips have helped me along the way.

- Start where you are – The budgeting process is no place for wishful thinking. Developing a workable budget must begin with your current situation. An honest budget will identify the pressure points on your finances and will show you where adjustments need to be made either on your income or your expenditures.
- Work as a team–Allow more than one family member to be involved in financial matters. Even if one partner has most of the responsibility for decision making, both partners should meet to discuss budgets and financial plans. The more involved each member is in the process, the more ownership he or she will take.
- Set goals–Put a dollar amount and time frame on each of your financial goals. If you don't take this step, you haven't established meaningful goals. Remember, goals are only goals when they are measurable and time specific. If you budget with the end in view, then individual decisions (either about increasing your income or decreasing your expenses) become easier.
- Write it down–The only way to get a better grip on your money is to have everything written down and planned out. Remind yourself of large expenditures. Put a note on your calendar at least three months before you have to

---

NOTES

pay a large bill like an insurance premium. Planning ahead for major expenses can keep you from dipping into savings too frequently or using credit unwisely.

- Become a saver–Begin a savings fund. No matter how small, no matter how inadequate, a beginning is a beginning. Save all of your "new found" money. If you just made your last car payment, continue putting the money you were spending on the payments into a savings account.

- Keep credit cards at home–Keep your expenditures in the present by using cash or a debit card. Use credit cards only for emergencies or when your plan is to pay them off every month.

- Rethink your shopping style–If you're an impulse buyer, set the rule for yourself that you can't buy something you want until you check to see if you can get it cheaper somewhere else.

- Remember your weakness–Set very specific budget amounts in "areas of weakness," that is, areas where you tend to overspend. Keep a running total of expenses as you spend the money instead of waiting until the end of the month to tally up what you have spent. This reminds you just how much you're spending on soda, candy, or coffee as you go.

- Focus on your goals —The key to making financial plans work is to keep your goals in mind. These goals are, in fact, the driving force. If one of your goals is to live financially free so that you can honor God, and you are able to keep that particular goal in focus, you will be better able to cope with the inevitable challenges of living on a budget. I encourage you to begin today. Redirect your monthly finances based upon your plan, your desires, and your budget.

NOTES

For Application

Step 1 - Establish Stewardship Goals
Step 2 - Organize Your Family Finances
Step 3 - Calculate Your Family's Net Worth
Step 4 - Figure out Your Current Income and Expenses
Step 5 - Create a Realistic Budget and Monitor Your Income/Spending

Step 1 - Establish Stewardship Goals

Goal planning suggestions

Using the suggestions below, identify your goals and list a few plans to reach them using the Goal Planning Worksheet on the following page. Be sure to add the cost including inflation, time frames and any helpers/advisors who can assist you for accomplishing these goals. You may want to refer to the, "Getting a Fix on Your Current Position" mini-test for goal ideas.

GOAL	TIME FRAMES	HELPERS/ ADVISORS
1. Establish a budget	3 mos.	Family/Friend
2. Get out of debt	6 months	Pastor
3. Plan and invest for retirement	1 year	Banker
4. Begin an emergency savings plan	2 years	Accountant
5. Reduce your mortgage interest rate	5 years	Financial Planner
6. Lower your insurance costs	10 years	Insurance Broker
7. Diversify your investments and add growth	20 years	Stock Broker
8. Save for a major purchase	30 years	Estate Planner
9. Create/revise your will(s) or estate plan	Annually	
10. Be involved in ministry		
11. Save for special needs for child/grandchild		
12. Make a career change		
13. Save for education (yours, child's, or grandchild's)		

Goal Planning Worksheet

Use this worksheet to begin developing your own set of goals. Don't hesitate to refer to this Chapter to get yours started.

GOALS	PLANS	COST	TIME FRAME	ADVISORS

1. _____ a._____ _____ _____ _____

  _____ b._____ _____ _____ _____

  _____ c._____ _____ _____ _____

2. _____ a._____ _____ _____ _____

  _____ b._____ _____ _____ _____

  _____ c._____ _____ _____ _____

3. _____ a._____ _____ _____ _____

  _____ b._____ _____ _____ _____

  _____ c._____ _____ _____ _____

4. _____ a._____ _____ _____ _____

  _____ b._____ _____ _____ _____

  _____ c._____ _____ _____ _____

5. _____ a._____ _____ _____ _____

  _____ b._____ _____ _____ _____

  _____ c._____ _____ _____ _____

6. _____ a._____ _____ _____ _____

  _____ b._____ _____ _____ _____

  _____ c._____ _____ _____ _____

Step 2 - Organize your Family Finances

A lack of organization can hinder your ability to effectively and efficiently complete the remaining budgeting steps. The system that you use to organize your financial data can be a manual paper system or a financial computer software program. The most important thing is that whatever system you choose is one that works for you. To begin your organization process, gather all current information about the source and amounts of your income, monthly/quarterly/annual bills (paid and unpaid), savings, investments, insurance, real estate, pension plans, etc. You also need to have updated contact information on your bank, mortgage holder, CPA, stockbroker, financial planner, credit card companies, etc. in case you need to contact representatives at these institutions. Put all of this data in one location and have it available at all times.

Step 3 - Calculate Your Family's Net Worth

Calculating Your Net Worth

The best way to measure your current resources is to calculate your net worth, which is a combination of your assets and liabilities. Fill in the blanks with the most current information that you have.

Use this worksheet to achieve the following:
- Assess your current financial situation
- Assist in your budgeting and goal setting process
- Assist your professional advisors
- Help you chart your progress

Date: _____

What I/We Own

What I/We Owe

Liquid Assets

Liabilities

Checking Account Balance_____

Credit Card Balances_____

Bank Savings Balance_____

Home Mortgage _____

Cash Value of Life Insurance_____

Investment Real
            Estate Mortgages _____

Other_____

Estate Mortgages _____

Other_____

Auto/RV/Boat Loans_____

Other_____

College Loans_____

Taxes Owed _____

Investment Assets

Other_____

Mutual Funds _____

Other_____

Stocks_____

Real Estate Investments_____

Total Liabilities

Antiques & Collectibles_____

Total Liabilities _____

Retirement Accounts _____

Other_____

Personal Assets – (current market value of each)

Residence   _____
Home Furnishings _____
Vehicles   _____
Boat/RV's   _____
Other   _____

Assets - Liabilities = Net Worth	
Total Assets	_____
Total Liabilities	- _____
Net Worth	= _____

Total Assets

Step 4 - Figure Out Your Current Income and Expenses

CURRENT INCOME AND EXPENSE WORKSHEET

Calculate your current level of income, expenses and savings in order to construct a cash flow analysis, which shows you if you are living within your means and what your spending priorities are. This information can be used to determine your estimated expenses for your new budget in step five of this application section.

<u>CURRENT INCOME</u> (One month)

Gross Income (total of all paychecks)	$ _____	
Investment and other Income	$ _____	
Total	$ _____	(1)

<u>DEDUCTIONS</u> (Less Tithes, Offerings, Payroll Deductions)

Tithes	$ _____	
Offerings	$ _____	
Payroll deductions (taxes, Social Security, etc.)	$ _____	
Retirement deductions (IRA, 401(k), etc.)	$ _____	
Health insurance premiums	$ _____	
Total	$ _____	(2)

TOTAL NET TAKE HOME PAY (1 – 2 = A) $ _____ (A)

<u>VARIABLE EXPENSES</u> – These are paid on a periodic basis. Estimate your current expenses over a 3-12 month period and divide it by that number of months to calculate your monthly cost. Be sure to include all payments that you currently make by credit card and debit card.

Category	Estimated Cost for 3 Months (divided by three) = Monthly Cost	
Homeowner's insurance	$ _____	$ _____
Furnishings/Appliances	$ _____	$ _____
Clothing/Shoes	$ _____	$ _____
Laundry/Dry cleaning	$ _____	$ _____
Auto repairs/Tires	$ _____	$ _____
Auto insurance	$ _____	$ _____
Other transportation	$ _____	$ _____
Books/Subscriptions	$ _____	$ _____
School tuition/Tudors	$ _____	$ _____
Vacations/Short trips	$ _____	$ _____
Property taxes	$ _____	$ _____
Self-employment taxes	$ _____	$ _____
Losses (fire/storm/theft)	$ _____	$ _____
Medical	$ _____	$ _____
Dental/Optical	$ _____	$ _____
Prescriptions	$ _____	$ _____
Life/Disability insurance	$ _____	$ _____
Other	$ _____	$ _____
Total Variable Expenses	$ _____	$ _____

<u>FIXED EXPENSES</u> – These are expenses that are paid monthly. For some expenses you may need to add the estimated expenses for three months and divide it by three to calculate the average monthly cost. Include all payments that you make by credit card and debit card.

Category	Estimated Cost for 3 Months (divided by three) = Monthly Cost	
Groceries	$ _____	$_____
Dining Out	$ _____	$_____
Mortgage/Rent	$ _____	$_____
Gas/Electricity/Oil	$ _____	$_____

Water/Sewer/Garbage	$ _____	$ _____
Household Supplies	$ _____	$ _____
Phone	$ _____	$ _____
TV/Computer Line	$ _____	$ _____
Misc. Household Items	$ _____	$ _____
Auto gas/oil/parking	$ _____	$ _____
Auto Loan Payments	$ _____	$ _____
Movies/Sports/Hobbies/Clubs	$ _____	$ _____
Babysitters	$ _____	$ _____
Gifts (birthday,wedding, etc.)	$ _____	$ _____
Childcare/Day Care	$ _____	$ _____
Beauty/Barber/Personal	$ _____	$ _____
School lunches/Allowances	$ _____	$ _____
Alimony/Child Support	$ _____	$ _____
Work-related Expenses	$ _____	$ _____
Bank Fees	$ _____	$ _____
Other	$ _____	$ _____
Total Variable Expenses	$ _____	$ _____

TOTAL OF ALL VARIABLE & FIXED EXPENSES $ _____
NET TAKE HOME PAY, MINUS EXPENSES (can be + or -) $ _____

• If your take home pay is greater than your expenses you are living WITHIN YOUR MEANS, but you may not be saving money for emergencies and future goals.

• If your take home pay is less than your expenses then you are living ABOVE YOUR MEANS, probably going into debt using credit cards and desperately need to lower some of your expenses as you create a realistic budget.

MONTHLY SAVINGS (and non-deductible retirement)

Emergency fund savings $ _____
Short-term savings $ _____
Long-term savings $ _____
Retirement savings (not deducted from payroll) $ _____

TOTAL SAVINGS (_____% of A) $ _____

Step 5 - Create a Realistic Budget & Monitor Income/Spending

Here in step 5 you will find first, a sample budget to familiarize you with how it works, then a blank budget worksheet that follows for your personal use.

Sample Household Budget Worksheet

In this example we have used a total household income of $55,000, which includes some income from investment sources. The worksheet defines net take home pay as income minus tithes, offerings, and payroll deductions. The anticipated monthly expenses for each category are listed to provide some ideas about how the budget works, but your expenses will be based on your own priorities and the amount of money you have budgeted to spend. This budget worksheet is based upon the following expense goals for your net take home pay:

Debt Retirement = 20% Savings = 10% Living Expenses = 70%

(SAMPLE BUDGET)

Anticipated Income (One Month)	Detail Subtotal	Category Subtotal	
Earnings from employment (gross)	$4,300		
Other known income		300	
TOTAL ANTICIPATED INCOME (gross)		$4,600	**1**
Less Tithes, Offerings, Payroll Deductions			
Tithes		$460	
Offerings		75	
TOTAL TITHES AND OFFERINGS		$535	**2**
Payroll deductions (i.e. taxes, social security, etc.)	$425		
Retirement deductions (401(k), IRA)	300		
Health insurance premiums	115		
TOTAL PAYROLL DEDUCTIONS		$840	**3**
TOTAL NET TAKE HOME PAY (1-2-3=A)		$ 3,225	**A**
Anticipated Expenses (One Month)			
Food:			
Groceries	$380		
Dining out/miscellaneous	60		
TOTAL FOOD		$ 440	**4**

(SAMPLE BUDGET, CON'T)

Shelter and Home Maintenance:

Rent/mortgage	$750	
Gas/electricity/oil	70	
Water/sewer/garbage	50	
Misc. household supplies	15	
Phone/TV/computer line	75	
Insurance (homeowners/fire/flood)	50	
Furnishings/appliances	20	
Other purchases	20	
TOTAL SHELTER AND HOME MAINTENANCE		$1,050 **5**

Clothing:

Clothes/shoes	$40	
Laundry/dry cleaning/tailoring	10	
TOTAL CLOTHING		$50 **6**

Transportation:

Gas/oil/parking	$120	
Repairs/tires	25	
Auto insurance	100	
Other transportation	_____	
TOTAL TRANSPORTATION		$245 **7**

Education:

Books/subscriptions	$15	
Tuition/tutor	_____	
TOTAL EDUCATION		$15 **8**

Recreation:

Movies/sports/plays/clubs	$25	
Babysitters	20	
Gifts (birthdays, Christmas, etc.)	30	
Vacations/short trips/miscellaneous	40	
TOTAL RECREATION, AMUSEMENT, ETC.		$115 **9**

(SAMPLE BUDGET, CON'T)

Deductible Expenses:

Taxes (property, self-employment)	$125
Losses (fire, storm, theft)	_____
Medical/dental/optical/prescriptions	80

TOTAL DEDUCTIBLE EXPENSES $205 **10**

Other Expenses:

Childcare/day care	$_____
Beauty/barber/personal	40
Children: School lunches, allowances ...	20
Alimony/child support	_____
Work-related expenses	10
Life/Disability Insurance	40
Other	30

TOTAL OTHER EXPENSES $140 **11**

TOTAL ALL EXPENSES

(4+5+6+7+8+9+10+11=B) Goal:70% of A $ 2,260 **B**

DEBT RETIREMENT (One Month)

Vehicle payments	$ 350
Appliance payments	25
Furniture payments	50
Loan payments (not mortgages)	70
Credit card payments	150

TOTAL DEBT RETIREMENT Goal:20% of A $ 645 **12**

Savings (One Month)

Emergency fund	$ 100
Short-term goals	70
Long-term goals	150
Retirement (not deducted from paycheck) ..	_____

TOTAL SAVINGS Goal:10% of A $ 320 **13**

(SAMPLE BUDGET, CON'T)

TOTAL ALL EXPENSES, DEBT RETIREMENT, SAVINGS (B+12+13=C)

(EQUIVALENT TO, OR LESS THAN, TAKE HOME PAY) $ 3225 **C**

NET CASH (A-C=D) $ 0 **D**

If this budget feels tight to you, you're probably not alone. For those who have not written out a balanced budget before and just spent money each month using cash and credit, this activity may be a reality check about what you really can afford!

If this were my budget, the first thing that I would do to help create some more "breathing room" in my month would be to cut my savings to 5% and plow the other 5% into my debt payments to accelerate paying them off. Just look, once the appliance, credit card, loan, and furniture payments are gone (not including auto) you have literally "found" $270 to spend in other areas of your budget. There are some cost-saving suggestions in the chapter on spending that can help you create more room in your budget as well.

I recommend that you continue to save even when debt payments exist so that if an emergency comes up you don't have to go back into debt to take care of it. It also helps to begin learning the habit of saving even in a small way. Once your debt payments are gone, it is important to then increase your savings back to the 10% target or even possibly put some or all of the new-found funds into savings as well.

Household Budget Worksheet

Use this worksheet to list your income, subtract tithes and offerings, and payroll deductions to arrive at your total net take home pay. It is also used to list your anticipated monthly expenses for each category, based on your priorities and the amount of money you have budgeted to spend. This budget worksheet is based upon the following expense goals for your net take home pay:

Debt Retirement = 20%   Savings = 10%   Living Expenses = 70%

Guidelines for Developing a Monthly Household Budget

A budget is a road map for you to use to advance toward your goals. It will help you organize spending and provide you with peace of mind. By treating your household like a business, with income and expenses that must be managed, you will gain control of your financial situation with the flexibility to meet and cover both unexpected and planned expenses.

YOUR BUDGET WORKSHEET

	DETAIL SUBTOTAL	CATEGORY SUBTOTAL
ANTICIPATED INCOME (One Month)		
Earnings from employment (gross) ..	$_____	
Other known income..........................	_____	
TOTAL ANTICIPATED INCOME (gross)		$_____ 1
Less Tithes, Offerings, Payroll Deductions		
Tithes..	$_____	
Offerings...	_____	
TOTAL TITHES AND OFFERINGS		$_____ 2
Payroll deductions (i.e. taxes, social security, etc.)	$_____	
Retirement deductions (401(k), IRA)	_____	
Health insurance premiums...............	_____	
TOTAL PAYROLL DEDUCTIONS	$_____ 3	
TOTAL NET TAKE HOME PAY (1-2-3=A)		$_____ A
ANTICIPATED EXPENSES (One Month)		
Food:		
Groceries..	$_____	
Dining out/miscellaneous	_____	
TOTAL FOOD		$_____ 4
Shelter and Home Maintenance:		
Rent/mortgage	$_____	
Gas/electricity/oil...........................	_____	
Water/sewer/garbage......................	_____	

(Your Budget Worksheet Con't)

Misc. household supplies .... _____

Phone/TV/computer line .... _____

Insurance (homeowners/fire/flood) _____

Furnishings/appliances .... _____

Other purchases .... _____

TOTAL SHELTER AND HOME MAINTENANCE $ _____ 5

Clothing: ....

Clothes/shoes .... $_____

Laundry/dry cleaning/tailoring ...... _____

TOTAL CLOTHING $_____ 6

Transportation:

Gas/oil/parking .... $_____

Repairs/tires .... _____

Auto insurance .... _____

Other transportation .... _____

TOTAL TRANSPORTATION $ _____ 7

Education:

Books/subscriptions .... $_____

Tuition/tutors .... _____

TOTAL EDUCATION $ _____ 8

Recreation:

Movies/sports/plays/clubs .... $_____

Babysitters .... _____

Gifts (birthdays, Christmas, etc.) .. _____

Vacations/short trips/miscellaneous _____

TOTAL RECREATION, AMUSEMENT, ETC. $ _____ 9

Deductible Expenses:

Taxes (property, self-employment) $_____

Losses (fire, storm, theft) .... _____

Medical/dental/optical/prescriptions _____

TOTAL DEDUCTIBLE EXPENSES $ _____ 10

Other Expenses:

Childcare/day care .... $_____

Beauty/barber/personal .... _____

Children: School lunches, allowances _____

Alimony/child support .... _____

Work-related expenses .... _____

(Your Budget Worksheet Con't)

Life/Disability Insurance ....   _____

Other ....   _____

TOTAL OTHER EXPENSES $ _____ 11

TOTAL ALL EXPENSES

(4+5+6+7+8+9+10+11=B) Goal:70% of A $_____ **B**

DEBT RETIREMENT (One Month)

Vehicle payments .... $_____

Appliance payments.......................   _____

Furniture payments.......................   _____

Loan payments (not mortgages)....   _____

Credit card payments....................   _____

TOTAL DEBT RETIREMENT Goal:20% of A $ _____ 12

SAVINGS (One Month)

Emergency fund .... $_____

Short-term goals ....   _____

Long-term goals ....   _____

Retirement (not deducted from paycheck)   _____

TOTAL SAVINGS Goal:10% of A $ _____ 13

TOTAL ALL EXPENSES, DEBT RETIREMENT, SAVINGS (B+12+13=C)

(EQUIVALENT TO, OR LESS THAN, TAKE HOME PAY) $ _____ **C**

NET CASH (A-C=D) $ _____ **D**

Summary

1. If your total expenses (C) equal your take home pay (A) and (D)=0, your budget balances.

2. If your total expenses (C) are less than your take home pay (A) and (D)=$X, funds are available for discretionary expenses/investment.

3. If your total expenses (C) are more than your take home pay (A) and (D)=-($X), review your budget for needed expense reduction.

Monthly Budget Account Sheet

This sheet can be duplicated and used to record and monitor your monthly spending for each budget category after you have decided what your monthly budget should be in each category. The most efficient way to do use this tool is to transfer all expenses (cash, check, debit card, and credit card) to this sheet every 3-4 days. It works like your checkbook register.

Each budget category should have its own account sheet with the budgeted amount shown. As the money is spent, the balance is reduced and at any time during the month you will know whether you are sticking to your budget. If your expenses are greater than your budget estimates, you'll need to make some adjustments. You can either increase your income, raise the monthly budgeted amount, cut your spending elsewhere, or do a combination of these.

MONTH _____**BUDGET CATEGORY** _____

Date_____ Description and PurposePayment (-) $ Balance

Beginning Budget Balance _____

1. _____ _____ $_____ _____

2 _____ _____ $_____ _____

3. _____ _____ $_____ _____

4. _____ _____ $_____ _____

5 _____ _____ $_____ _____

6. _____ _____ $_____ _____

7. _____ _____ $_____ _____

8 _____ _____ $_____ _____

9. _____ _____ $_____ _____

10. _____ _____ $_____ _____

Difference between BUDGETED and ACTUAL expenses: $ _____

____ Overspent or ____ Underspent

Personal Finance Improvement Checklist

Use the checklist below to summarize the work you have done on your goals, budgeting, organization, etc. If there are any steps that you skipped, plan a time to go back and complete that activity.

____ Prayerfully complete the goal-setting worksheets with your immediate family.

____ Organize your financial files, investment accounts, insurance data, unpaid bills, etc. to help create your budget and conduct other financial planning with easy access.

____ Complete the "Calculating Your Net Worth" worksheet to determine your present worth, then plan to update it on annually.

____ Carefully determine your current income and expense levels as a first step to creating your budget.

____ Create an initial budget that is flexible. It will probably need to be adjusted over the next three to six months until it becomes realistic. Make a commitment to faithfully monitor your income and expenses to avoid spending leaks.

After you complete steps one through five, mark the tips below that will help you continue the process of improving your financial management.

____ Begin to live below your means (reduce food, insurance, utilities, car, and entertainment expense).

____ Kick bad spending habits.

____ Try the "Cash Management Method" if other budgeting approaches have failed.

____ Share your budget and goal plans with your spouse and children. Create areas of responsibility for each participant.

____ Create areas of responsibility in your budget and goals for each participant in your family to increase accountability, ownership, and success.

____ Consider using a computer program to help you manage your finances such as Microsoft Money, Quicken, etc.

Reflections on Goals and Budgeting

1. Proverbs has a lot to say about goals and plans. **Read Proverbs 15:22, 16:3, and 21:5** and reflect on your own situation. Have you been living paycheck to paycheck without a plan in place? What can you do today to apply the instruction about planning found in these verses? _____

   _____

   _____

   _____

2. Budgeting and goal setting are just empty activities if we don't stick to them. They take discipline and self-control to be successful according to **Proverbs 25:28**. Are you lacking self-control in these areas? Ask God to give you a new sense of purpose and a fire in your heart to achieve your goals and stick to your budget.

3. **Read Luke 14:28** and consider it a metaphor for budgeting and goal setting (or accomplishing anything else in life). How will you reach your goals or properly manage your finances if you don't first count the cost with the help of a budget? What thoughts does this scripture invoke in you? _____

   _____

   _____

   _____

4. As you begin to develop your goals, ask God for guidance and direction. Consider goals that are financial, spiritual, and for personal development. Are your motives for your list of goals in line with God's plan for your life or are they influenced by the World's views?_____

   _____

   _____

   _____

Prayer: *Lord, you instruct us to make plans that are based on wise counsel and that are committed to you. I confess that I have not been planning in that way (or at all). I ask for your forgiveness for my lack of discipline and I pledge today to begin a process of planning that is based on your guidance and direction. Help me to have the self-control necessary to achieve my goals and to stick to my budget. Amen.*

CHAPTER 4

Spending

*In order to find proper
balance in your spending,
the key question to ask yourself is
"Are your finances and your spending
in harmony with God's perspective
on money?"*

Our spending habits, positive and negative, have a great deal to do with our ability to achieve financial freedom. Many of the books written on financial freedom handle the issue of spending indirectly. When discussing spending, they cover budgeting and the proper handling of living expenses rather than tackling this key issue head on.

With all the easy credit available, we can always spend more than we make. This is a major trap, especially for young people. Most newlyweds have a limited financial base when they get married; yet, within three to four years, they attempt to equal or surpass their parents' standard of living. Because there are so many borrowing options, many young couples can quickly purchase houses, cars and other possessions — achieving nearly the same lifestyle that it took their parents 25 years to accomplish. Unfortunately, in the process of "keeping up with the Joneses," or attaining the standard of living they enjoyed while growing up, many young couples bury themselves in every imaginable kind of debt and end up in financial bondage.

"The Lord is my shepherd, I shall not be in want"

Psalm 23:1

Some people think that if they are "given credit" with generous limits or if they "qualify" for a loan, it is okay for them to spend it. "After all, if a bank thinks my financial situation is credit worthy, they know what they are doing."

NOTES

But this is not true. Because of the competitive nature of lending, many different banks & stores may be willing to issue you credit. In our culture, most people can receive more credit than they can ever repay.

My wife and I had been married only a few years when we found ourselves not only in debt, but bound because of our use and abuse of credit cards and consumer credit. Like so many young couples, we began our lives together excited about having our first home. We made purchases spontaneously without thought of how we would make payments. When an emergency came up, we were thankful to have a credit card to take up the slack. This pattern led us to increasing consumer debt, a fragile financial base and the pressure to pay back money owed while still pressed with daily expenses. The issues we faced were difficult, and we had few, if any, tools to handle them. The more pressure we experienced, the more we tried to feel good by buying things for our home and ourselves. As you can imagine, it didn't take long to get out of control. We felt helpless, embarrassed by our situation, and at odds with each other.

During this time our church began a series on biblical stewardship. As we learned what God had to say about financial priorities and money management, we realized we had not submitted to the Lord in this area of our lives. We were operating like owners, not as stewards like God intended.

Based on the teaching we received, we began to tithe and made a commitment to control our spending. We learned about budgeting, planning and saving. We learned we could be content in the Lord and in our growing relationship with one another. God was faithful to continue teaching us as we learned a new way to live.

Our journey has led to new choices and the development of new habits through some tough times of making mistakes and beginning again. Now we

---

NOTES

understand that the kind of financial freedom God intends for His children is far more than simply being debt free.

Another couple, Carol and Gary, go on spending sprees in an effort to get an emotional lift or a "feel good" response. They have placed themselves under the financial pressure of credit card debt by spending without planning. As you might imagine, this is not the most productive thing for them to do. The result of these shopping sprees is stress, blame, frustration, and feelings of resentment toward one another. More often than not, they lack the essentials needed to carry out their everyday life. Gary calls it a "cash flow" problem when money for gasoline, groceries and lunches is spent on expensive evenings partying with friends or purchasing electronic gadgets which soon lose their use. Because Carol and Gary like to spend, they find themselves in disagreement on how to spend their money, rather than whether or not to spend.

Mike and Cathy are a newly married couple with very different backgrounds and different issues when it comes to spending. Mike wants to avoid spending and fears debt of any kind. He wants to save any extra money. Cathy believes your bills should be paid first, but that money left over can be used for things you want or need. Cathy finds herself frequently frustrated because the subject is difficult for them to discuss, and she describes Mike as ultra-conservative or "tight" with their finances.

What do you see and feel as you read these stories? Notice how spending is a central issue, but each person has come into the situation with prior programming or habits which dictate his or her behavior. There is disagreement over how to spend and on what. It is clear that when spending is not planned and in control, it causes problems that can strain and destroy communication in marriage.

NOTES

Are You Overspending?

If you think that you're immune to overspending, I challenge you to evaluate the major purchases you have made during the last three years and consider the motivation behind each one. Did you make your decisions to meet a need or in an effort to achieve a particular standard of living?

Take the "Spending Quiz" at the end of the chapter to see if you have your spending habits under control. Before any significant financial freedom can be realized, or any lasting planning accomplished, it will help to identify how your spending patterns are established, what can be done to bring them into control, and what God's plan is for spending.

Prior Programming

Professionals who study human behavior say we have emotional "triggers" that, when stimulated, produce actions. Very often we are not consciously aware of these emotional triggers.

Emotional triggers are silent messengers from the past or present producing various behaviors that often keep us in old habit patterns. An emotional trigger can start with feeling lonely, move to the thought, "I will feel better if I am with people," and instead of calling a friend, you go shopping.

"Let us fix our eyes on Jesus, the author and the perfector of our faith..."

Heb. 12:2a

All kinds of things can trigger spending. In a world where advertising is targeted to associate spending with pleasure, Christians have to make an effort to understand what's going on in and around them in order to live purposefully in this area. It is worth taking the time to think through your personal spending habits, iso-

NOTES

late any "emotional triggers" that may be affecting you, and ask God to help you form healthy biblical patterns for spending. If we do not control our spending "triggers," they will often result in the following:

- Spending sprees that leave us with bills, guilt and negative financial consequences
- Stress and disagreement when sharing financial decisions with a partner
- Frustration and fear whenever facing a need to spend
- Debilitating indecision over what is appropriate and timely with regard to spending

Personal Habits

Personal spending habits can become patterns that keep us from moving toward real financial freedom. Sometimes we think that if all of our immediate bills are paid we can buy what we want. But this may not be true if we are spending without any plan for the future or spending when we have no savings as a backup. We live in a world where there is always something new. It takes a conscious effort not to care about what is newer and better than what we have. Many people have the habit of "recreational shopping," and it keeps them constantly tempted to spend spontaneously. God's plan is that we establish habits based upon His Word, have a plan, and save for the things we want and need.

Having and Maintaining Balance

In order to find the proper balance in your spending, the key question to ask yourself is "Are your finances and your spending habits in harmony with God's perspective on money?" It is important to realize that God is the owner and we are to manage. Here is what God tells us in His Word:

- Psalm 24:1 tells us that, "The earth is the Lord's and everything in it."

NOTES

- Psalm 50:10 says, "For every animal of the forest is mine, and the cattle on a thousand hills."
- Haggai 2:8 says, "The silver is mine, and the gold is mine declares the Lord Almighty." Anything we think we own actually belongs to God, and He graciously allows us to manage His riches.
- Luke 14:28 says, "Suppose one of you wants to build a tower. Will he not first sit down and estimate the cost to see if he has enough money to complete it?" This passage encourages us to be wise stewards.
- In Matthew 25, Jesus tells a parable about three stewards. He commends the two stewards who invest their master's money in order to earn more. In the same way, as wise stewards of God's money, we must put it to work utilizing the resources that are available to us.

Why is spending such a big issue? For a Christian spending is a big issue because it is one of the quickest ways we can get off track, fall back into old behavior patterns, and get into serious financial trouble before we know it.

Wise Spending Principles

1. Don't buy what you can't afford. We are bombarded daily with ads that try to convince us that ownership is power, prestige, and prosperity. Advertisers tell us we need to look better, be happier and healthier, or live like royalty. Pray for wisdom and discernment to become a disciplined spender. Don't let others and their spending habits dictate yours. Certain people (you know who they are) bring out the big spender in you. Do something else with them besides shopping.

2. Pay yourself first. One of the quickest ways to improve your finances is to "pay yourself first" by committing a percentage of your income to a savings account before you pay a single bill. Committing to a deliberate and systematic savings program removes the temptation to misuse or waste money you will appreciate more later. When you apply the 70/20/10 budgeting formula that we discussed in the previous chapter, you are essentially "paying yourself first."

3. Time really does equal money. Have you heard the saying, "Money makes money, and the money money makes, makes money." This is describing the power of compounding interest. With compound interest, the initial investment and its interest earn more interest. The longer and earlier you are able to get money working for you, the more financial rewards you will experience.

4. Money can create a whole new set of problems. Many people are duped into believing that having more money will solve all their problems. The primary dangers you face by having more money are that money can eventually possess you, creating a false sense of security. Furthermore, it won't matter how much money you have if your spending habits are bad. Both of these negative effects can lessen your faith in Christ, the only One who can give you genuine purpose, meaning, happiness, and protection in life.

5. Consumption equates to lost opportunities. Any time you spend dollars unwisely or unnecessarily, you lose multiple future dollars because the money you spent could have grown in an investment account. Financial maturity is being able to give up today's small pleasures for tomorrow's larger benefits. Delayed gratification creates more opportunities.

6. Adjust your lifestyle as you age. To achieve true financial freedom, we must learn how to limit our style of living voluntarily. This means that you

---

NOTES

should not live the lifestyle of the rich when you are not rich — advertisers and societal standards are certainly no help! Many very wealthy people live middle-class lifestyles and don't seem to suffer for it. They understand that maintaining a limited lifestyle is what allowed them to build their wealth in the first place — and they did not increase their lifestyles as their wealth grew.

As your earning capacity increases and your investments begin to pay off, remember to slow down! It will take discipline to limit your style of living, but that may be the only way to achieve financial freedom.

Benefits of Reduced Spending

As you implement a spending reduction strategy, you will reap the benefits for years to come. For every $1,000 per year ($83 per month) that you shave from your spending, you gain that much opportunity to save for your future. The illustration below gives a good picture of the benefits of reducing your spending and directing those funds into a retirement account.

For every $83 per month that you can reduce your spending and put into a retirement savings account earning 7% interest compounded monthly, you'll have this much money:

5 years	10 Years	20 Years	40 Years
$5,966	$14,423	$43,409	$218,726

Practical Ways to Control or Reduce Spending

At this point, you may be wondering how it's possible to reduce your spending. Maybe you have already put serious thought to your spending habits and you have cut back as much as you know how, but it's still not enough. There are

NOTES

only a few ways to save $5,000, but thousands of ways to save $5.00. Following are some practical tips to give you ideas for ways to reduce spending in several categories.

Household cost-cutting suggestions
- Plan shopping in advance and buy only what you plan
- Find the best values - join a wholesale superstore
- Use fans instead of air conditioning
- Join or form a baby-sitting club
- See movies at a discount theater or go during the matinee rates
- Shop at garage sales, flea markets, and discount stores
- Return items that don't hold up through the warranty period
- Write letters or use e-mail instead of calling
- Barter and/or exchange services with family, friends, or neighbors
- Sew some items for the home and make handmade gifts
- Cut your children's hair instead of paying a salon
- Control heat/air thermostat — lower it in winter, raise it in summer, put it on a timer

Save on auto expenses
- Buy used vehicles
- Join a carpool
- Wash the car and change the oil yourself
- Increase the deductible on your car insurance

Food saving ideas
- Eat out more frugally

NOTES

- Shop at bulk food stores
- Plant a garden — can and freeze for the winter
- Shop the stores with the best bargains
- Avoid buying prepared snacks or convenience foods
- Look for savings on day-old bakery products
- Stick to your shopping list to avoid impulse buying
- Buy store-brand or generic-brand products and use coupons
- Buy less cereal — supplement with oatmeal, breads, homemade granola, fruit
- Cook in quantity — freeze meals to avoid fast-food nights.
- Consider 2-3 meatless evening meals each week
- Leave children home when you shop

Ways to save on clothes

- Plan your wardrobe before going shopping
- Shop during sales, and take advantage of off-season sales
- Avoid fad or trendy clothes when possible
- Buy and sell at garage sales
- Take care of your clothes
- Shop for some items at discount and thrift stores
- Return clothes that are the wrong size, style, or color
- Buy quality items that look better and last longer
- Learn to sew
- Avoid dry-cleanables

Ways to save on insurance

- Educate yourself on the variety of options available

NOTES

- Request estimates from several companies and compare prices
- Adjust deductible amounts to reduce your premiums
- Ask about discounts for things like burglar and smoke alarms
- Use the same insurer for different policies if a discount is offered
- Avoid unnecessary or duplicate insurance
- Buy "term" life insurance over "cash value" insurance and invest the difference

The average American spends 10% of their income on insurance coverage. Many people are over insured or pay too much for their coverage. Complete the insurance worksheet at the end of the chapter to identify a target for your life insurance needs.

Teaching Children about Spending

Have you ever seen a child in a grocery store begging and pleading for that candy bar, or they are in the toy section at the department store and clutching a package with "please, can I have it?" emerging as a desperate whine from their lips? We have all observed this and some of us probably experience that with our own children. Unfortunately, it is easiest to give in, especially if it is just a small thing, rather than listen to the whining or to avoid a scene in front of other shoppers. Why do children feel that they can badger their parents about these spontaneous and frivolous purchases? Where do they get the idea that we should give in to their purchasing whims? Well, obviously, part of the problem is that our children are bombarded by television commercials telling them that these are things that they "need." Another part of the problem are the parents who give in on enough occasions that their kids learn to persist.

Going shopping is an excellent training ground for teaching children

NOTES

about spending. If children can observe that we are shopping with a purpose and from a list, then we can help them understand that this is not a recreational activity. If you are able to plan your shopping in advance, I suggest that you involve the child in making the shopping list and then have him or her help you to check the things off the list while you are at the store. There may also be opportunities during this planning time to include on the list something that the child has

"Those who live according to the sinful nature have their minds set on what that nature desires; but those who live in accordance with the spirit, have their minds set on what the spirit desires."
Romans 8:5

expressed a desire for. That is the time that you would have him or her take funds from their "spending" or "saving" bank containers. If they don't have any money left in their bank, then their item does not go on the list.

Some parents also discuss the rules for shopping before they go into the store. The rule is, "Do not ask for anything." Then discuss with them what the consequences will be if they do ask. It is not productive to buy something for the child at the end of the shopping list because "they were on their best behavior." That reinforces the "if I'm good.....then I get...." mentality

rather than teaching them that they are on best behavior because it is the right thing to do. Of course, this is a "perfect world" scenario, where the personality of the child is not factored in. But, it is a starting place to help you think ahead to the spending patterns that you may be teaching your children or grandchildren.

Common Money Management Mistakes to Avoid[5]

With all the easy credit available, we can always spend more than we

---

NOTES

make. This is a major trap. The drive to "keep up with the Joneses" also exists for many of us. Easy credit coupled with the temptation to keep up appearances leads to financial trouble in a hurry. It is even easier to get into trouble when these money management mistakes are occurring in our lives.

1. **No spending plan.** Without a plan you are prone to spend impulsively, use credit unwisely, and end up in debt. Create your plan together with your spouse after discussion, prayer, and counsel.

2. **No cash reserve.** A family should have a reserve for unexpected emergencies (three months of expenses or income is a typical rule of thumb).

3. **Too much use of credit.** When handled correctly, credit can be good. Too often credit is used to purchase something you really can't afford.

4. **Poor use of extra money.** When you receive a bonus, inheritance, or tax refund, plan for its use in the same way you plan for other income. Before splurging, consider paying off debt, investing in education, or set up cash reserves for future purchases.

5. **No planning for large expenses.** You have large financial obligations looming in the future that you are presently unaware of. Planning for taxes, insurance premiums, car repairs, new appliances, or unexpected expenses (like a hot water heater) is necessary if you expect to be able to avoid using credit when these circumstances arise.

6. **Underestimating the cost of ownership.** The more "things" you acquire the more you can expect to spend on maintenance and repairs. Appliances, stereos, lawnmowers, furnaces, etc. are costly to maintain.

---

[5] Becoming Money Wise, Ronald Chewning, Concordia Publishing House, 1998, page 71.

NOTES

7. **Spending leaks.** Many people are prone to buying on impulse. Many times the items are small, but they all add up. The best way to avoid this is to reduce the opportunities for spending. Shop with a purpose, set time limits, research the item you need to purchase and wait 24 hours before buying.

8. **Careless shopping habits.** We live in a society that promotes everything imaginable, and we are told through advertisements that our lives are not complete unless we own it all. The best way to resist the tactics of sales people and avoid falling prey to this type of materialism is to stick to your budget.

9. **Not saving small amounts.** If all you can save is small amounts, don't get discouraged. Small expenditures add up, and so do small savings.

10. **Can't-wait attitude.** Some people are pressured to feel that it is mandatory to have it all now. During your youth is the time to develop patience and work on the "save now, buy later" attitude. Delayed gratification is a healthy principle for everyone to learn.[5]

11. **Confusion about needs, wants, and desires.** There is a vast difference between needs, wants, and desires. Needs are the purchases necessary to provide your basic requirements such as food, clothing, a job, home, and medical care. Wants involve choices about the quality of goods to be used. Desires are choices that should be made only out of surplus funds after all other obligations have been met. God promised to meet your needs and some of your desires, but you can't have all of your "wants."

NOTES

For Application

Personal Finance Improvement Checklist

____   Determine where your money is being spent and reduce spending in the appropriate areas.

____   Apply cost-cutting suggestions for food, clothing, cars, and new purchases.

____   Review your current insurance policies. Are you over or under insured?

____   Complete the Life Insurance Worksheet in this section to establish a target for your current situation.

____   Begin shopping with a list and a budget. Think twice about impulse buys at the cash register. Kick bad spending habits.

____   Make time to involve your children in planning the shopping list if you must take them shopping with you. Become aware of the spending habits that you are teaching them.

____   Track your spending by using a notepad or computer program to record purchases and keeping every receipt.

____   Complete the Spending Quiz and identify your shopping patterns. Write goals to improve your spending habits.

The Spending Quiz: (Be brutally honest with yourself!)   (Circle One)

1) Shopping for me is therapy.	True False
2) I have credit-card debt and pay interest on it.	True False
3) Many of my credit card charges are for discretionary items (items that are not absolutely necessary for survival).	True False
4) Often I buy little things that I want, on impulse, that were not on my shopping list. (This can happen at the grocery store, the shopping mall, a gift shop, etc.)	True False
5) I/we have house and/or car payments that really stretch our income.	True False
6) I/we have purchased new furniture and/or appliances or other items this past year on a promotional plan that promised "No interest or payments until _____."	True False
7) I/we own at least two of the following items that we have purchased on credit within the past two years: home or car stereo; DVD, VCR, TV; Play Station or other video games; cell phone; any kitchen "gadget" appliance; recreational items (boat or personal watercraft, skis or boards, motorcycle, bike, guns, hobby stuff, motor home, etc.).	True False

8) I/we buy a lot of CDs and videos and/or we love going to movies, concerts, and sporting events for which we often purchase tickets.	True False
9) I have purchased new clothes within the past month even though my closet is already pretty full.	True False
10) I/we love dining out, and do so at least once a week often using our credit card (not counting work-related entertainment expense or work lunches).	True False

Results: The more "true" answers you have, the more your spending habits and patterns are out of control.

Life Insurance Worksheet

Here's a "Life Insurance Worksheet" that can help you determine if you have the proper amount, or if you need less or more.

Key factors in considering your insurance needs:
- family's financial needs
- health
- work insurance

- age & gender
- number of children
- special needs

- occupation
- educational needs
- income of surviving spouse

Life insurance proceeds are typically used for:
- Paying off a home mortgage or other debts through a decreasing term policy
- Providing lump-sum payments to children when they reach a specified age
- Providing education or income to children/grandchildren
- Making a charitable bequest after death
- Providing retirement income & savings
- Establishing regular income for survivors & an estate plan
- Making estate and death tax payments

CURRENT NEEDS
1. Mortgage balance pay-off $ _____ 1

2. Debt pay-off $ _____ 2

3. College Education (present/future) $ _____ 3

4. Burial Expenses $ _____ 4

TOTAL CURRENT NEEDS (1+2+3+4) $ _____ A

INCOME NEEDS

5. Present annual living costs $ _____ 5

6. Spouse's current income   D $ _____ 6

7. Additional income needed   (5-6) = $ _____ 7
    Divide line 3 by .07% (the current interest rate) $ _____ A
(B = how much needs to be invested to create needed income)

TOTAL DOLLARS NEEDED (A + B) $ _____ C

LIQUID ASSETS AVAILABLE $ _____ D
      (Life insurance, retirement plans, CDs, stocks, bonds, etc.)

ADDITIONAL LIFE INSURANCE NEEDED (C - D = E) $ _____ E

Reflections on Spending

1. Evaluate your spending habits and triggers. Take an inventory of the times you usually like to shop and spend and ask God to reveal if you are shopping/spending to compensate for other negative things or feelings in your life. As God reveals this to you, confess it to Him and ask him for relief from these impulses. Decide to discipline yourself when you are feeling the impulse to spend outside of your plan.

_____

_____

_____

2. Do you feel trapped by your spending habits? Does changing them seem impossible to you? Read John 8:34-36 and Romans 8:12-15 and claim the promise that Christ will bring you freedom through a life in Him and that you do not have to be a slave to unhealthy habits.

3. Unhealthy habits, including spending habits, are often a compensation for negative experiences, thoughts, or feelings in our lives. Galatians 5:16-17 says that we can overcome unhealthy habits when we live by the Spirit. Are you spending to compensate for something else? How can you apply this truth to your life? _____

_____

_____

_____

4. Additional Scriptures for review and reflection:
    Romans 7: 15-25 and 8:5-9, Philippians 4:11-13 & 19, II Corinthians 9:8,
    Hebrews 13:5-6

Prayer: Lord, I confess that I have been living by the flesh and have not thought to submit my spending habits to you. Please show me the root of this unhealthy habit. Heal me by your Holy Spirit in those areas where I seem to be compensating for something negative. I commit today to put you in that empty place in my life that has been filled with the need to spend and to begin to live in the Spirit according to Romans 8:13. Amen.

Debt Management

Make the decision that today you will pay on a cash basis to cease robbing your future to pay for the past.

Most Americans live on the edge. Our "consumer mentality" and "capitalistic system" demand that we spend money on an ever-increasing array of goods and services. Think of cell phones, Internet hook-ups, and cable TV. It is not unusual for a household to spend $150 a month or more on these three things alone (not including the initial purchase price of the equipment). These were virtually non-existent a few years ago and now many think of them as indispensable.

> *"Don't run up debts, except for the huge debt of love you owe each other."*
> Romans 13:8
> (The Message)

Some of us, while saving for retirement and/or our children's education, realize that we are not saving near enough. Car and house payments, along with credit cards and monthly necessities leave our finances maxed out.

If this is you, or even a worse version than what I have described above, you probably need to do a serious gut check. This chapter will explain some specific steps you can take to help you move away from financial bondage and enter into financial freedom.

As a young man, I began managing my personal finances with very little plan in place and with the "prior programming" that some debt is inevitable. Most of what I knew and practiced came from observing my mother as she managed her small single-parent income and met the needs as I was growing up. She relied heavily on credit cards even though she was faithful to give offerings as

---

NOTES

the Lord prompted. Rather than being the manager of debt, it managed her. When I got married and tried to use the same system of management for our newly established household, I quickly discovered that staying ahead by transferring and juggling debt was the fastest possible way to get behind.

To have and manage debt takes some understanding of what debt is and a plan for having only the kind of debt which provides something of greater worth than the outstanding balance.

What Debt Is and Is Not

Once you get your spending under control, you have to get out of debt to have financial freedom. What would your financial health, cash flow, savings plan, and giving be like if you had no consumer debt?

My definition of debt may be a little different from what you have heard or read in the past, but after some analysis I hope it will make sense to you. *You are in debt when you are one or more payments past due on an account, when the amount of the debt is greater than the asset value of the item(s) purchased with that debt, or when you borrow for depreciating items.*

For example, if you have a mortgage on your home, but the value of that home is greater than the amount of the mortgage and you are current on your monthly payments, you are not in debt in this definition. On the other hand, if you purchase a car and the amount of the loan you take out to pay for it is greater than the depreciated value of the car at any time, you are in debt.

From a biblical perspective, if you choose to co-sign for another individual, you are in debt. The reason for this is that you have no control over the payment of that particular debt and may, at any time, be required to make payments that are outside of your plan. When you co-sign, your freedom is contingent

NOTES

upon the other person's ability and integrity to make the payments. You have established a contingent liability, which will show on your credit report when that co-signature is recorded with any credit bureau or agency. According to the Word of God, co-signing is prohibited.

My son, if you have put up security for your neighbor. You have been trapped by what you said, ensnared by the words of your mouth, then do this... Go humble yourself; plea with your neighbor...free yourself. (Prov. 6:1-3)

One of the immediate questions you may ask yourself is, "How in the world do I buy a car if I am in debt when it depreciates?" The key is to try to purchase with cash. If that's not possible, then try to save enough to make a significant down payment on the car. With a healthy down payment, you can structure the repayment of the balance in such a way that the outstanding balance of the loan is never greater than the depreciated value of the car. This strategy can be accomplished with careful planning. If you follow these steps, you are not in debt on that car as long as the monthly payments are kept current.

How People Get Into Debt

You may end up in debt as a result of circumstances beyond your control, such as an accident, illness, job loss, etc. However, most debt occurs for one or more of the following reasons:

DESIRE & IMPULSE

Desiring things you don't need, and impulsively purchasing things you think you must have, can lead to unwanted debt. Our society pressures us into wanting things now and our culture says we deserve them. God promises to give us our needs but not all of our greeds. Self-indulgence can be identified by one

---

NOTES

or more of the following things:

- purchasing without to regard to utility
- living a lavish lifestyle without the funds to support it
- consistently trading cars and appliances for newer models
- impulsively purchasing things just because they are "on sale"
- filling closet after closet with clothes, shoes, and accessories that are seldom or never worn

"The world and its desires pass away, but the man who does the will of God lives forever."
1 John 2:17

Because we desire more than we can afford, we fall into the trap of using credit to get it. Luke 12:15 says, "Watch out! Be on your guard against all kinds of greed; a man's life does not consist in the abundance of his possessions."

SELF-DECEPTION

It is easy to deceive ourselves into believing we need something and convincing ourselves we need it now. Retails stores, banks and lending agencies make it easy and convenient to get almost anything for a few dollars down and many "easy" payments — sometimes even bribing us with cash-back up front.

LACK OF LEARNING

Many people fail to take the necessary time to learn basic money management skills. A class on how to balance a checkbook or how to use credit cards correctly would be a huge benefit. Prov. 19:20 encourages us to "listen to advice and accept instruction, and in the end you will be wise."

NOTES

LACK OF PLANNING

Without goals, budgets, and restraints you are susceptible to impulse buying. Having long-range goals will give you the motivation to forego immediate, unnecessary desires. Solomon tells us in Proverbs14: 15, "A simple man believes anything, but a prudent man gives thought to his steps." Planning will solve many poor spending habits and resolve debt issues.

DOUBTING GOD'S PROVISION

Impatience, narrow-mindedness and a lack of faith in God to meet your needs can cause you to doubt that God will provide. Remember, God has His own timetable, and sometimes He says "no." When it comes to your needs, give Him an opportunity to meet them before you force the issue and try to get it yourself.

EASY CREDIT/MINIMUM PAYMENTS

Credit card companies prefer that we pay the minimum amount so they can charge us more interest. By only paying the minimum, we fall prey to paying interest on things purchased in the past, and immediate interest on any new purchases. Look at the chart at the end of chapter to see how long it will take to pay off a credit card balance using only the minimum payment due.

SHOP THERAPY

Some people spend money or go on buying binges to get out of a depressed mood. There may not even be a reason for the purchase, except that it helps emotionally. If you are prone to this, find something else to bring purpose and meaning into your life. If you must go shopping, go without your wallet.

NOTES

Symptoms of Financial Problems

As hard as they try to break the habit some people are addicted to spending and debting. It becomes a chronic problem that starts to interfere with other aspects of their lives.

Symptoms of financial problems show up in some of the ways listed below and can affect people physically, mentally, emotionally, and spiritually, leading to problems at work and with family and friends.

- Failure to pay off credit card balances
- Failure to set aside emergency funds
- Failure to keep an adequate balance on your checking/savings account
- Using savings to pay credit card bills
- Using advances from one credit card to pay off another
- Being past due with basic living expenses like rent or utilities
- Taking advances on checks
- Avoiding the mail

Consequences of Being in Debt

Unreasonable debt can have devastating effects on the financial future of one's family, produce tension and turmoil among family members, break up a marriage, and cause health problems. When debt is out of control, excessive funds need to be channeled to pay interest and principal to creditors. The problem of debt escalates because the loan's compounding interest works against the borrower. One alarming statistic estimates that nearly one-half of all Americans owe more than they own.

NOTES

DEBT CAN CAUSE DAMAGED RELATIONSHIPS

Your debt is too high if it causes anxiety and problems in your home or in your relationship with God. Our spiritual lives can be negatively affected when money issues monopolize our time, energy and conversation. Relationships and things more important than money are no longer the priority they should be. Our prayer lives, Bible study and church attendance may suffer or be ignored. We can't use our God-given resources as God directs us because we already owe it to others. We are unable to give to God or others as we wish when enslaved by excessive debt.

DEBT CAN JEOPARDIZE YOUR FUTURE

Through debt, some people lose their sense of reality. Using debt can deceive us into believing that we have more money than we do. When we live in a home owned primarily by the bank, filled with furniture paid for on installment plans, with a garage containing one or more vehicles owned in large part by banks, we can be duped into believing we are living the American dream. But in reality, by financing them we are jeopardizing our future. Having too much debt can drastically reduce a family's ability to save for the future, prepare for unforeseen emergencies, and respond to giving opportunities.

DEBT CAN CREATE LOST OPPORTUNITIES

Debt is both an opportunity loss and a financial loss. The more debt you have, the less investment potential you have. Debt causes your asset base to depreciate rather than appreciate. For example, if you pay monthly interest expenses, that is money lost forever. If that money were invested in a growth mutual fund, it would produce a healthy return. The opportunity cost would be

NOTES

huge. Your goal should be to get your money working for you instead of against you, for the work of God instead of being placed in the hands of creditors.

God's Attitude about Debt

Understanding God's attitude about debt is important. He says little about what we buy with borrowed money but goes in depth into the requirement to repay. The principle found in Proverbs is basic to Christian financial management. *"Honor the Lord with your wealth, with the firstfruits of all your crops; then your barns will be filled to overflowing, and your vats will brim over with new wine."* (Prov. 3:9-10) Clearly, our testimony is connected to how we handle our finances. We must be careful to honor God by being faithful to His principles. We should not allow mismanagement to damage our reputation so that we can't effectively testify and lead people to the Lord.

When is it Acceptable to Borrow?

All borrowing is not the same. Most business owners must operate by borrowing. If you become unemployed or have an accident, you may be in a situation where borrowing is your only option (hopefully after much prayer and thought). Improper borrowing is debt that is impulsive, discretionary, and unnecessary. If you can make a higher return on your investment than it costs to borrow, it makes sense to incur a liability. From an economic, comfort, and tax perspective, borrowing to purchase a home makes sense. The worst use of borrowing is to purchase perishables that are consumed — this is debt.

Reducing Debt

If you find yourself in a situation where your debt is out of balance and needs

NOTES

to be reduced to regain financial freedom, there are specific actions you can take.

1. Take a clear-minded look at what you actually owe. Using the "My Present Debt Load" worksheet at the end of this chapter, determine which debts carry the highest interest rate and which ones have the most significant impact on your cash flow. Typically, consumer debt and credit cards charge the highest interest rates and should be first targeted for elimination. Here are five approaches to debt reduction:

a. Eliminate the highest interest rate accounts first by doubling up your payments on those accounts, while maintaining the minimum payments on everything else.

b. Pay off the largest debt first by making any extra payment amount you can while maintaining the minimum payments on the other debts.

c. A more rewarding way to prepay debt may be to eliminate the smallest bills first and work up to the largest or highest interest rate debts.

d. Contact each creditor and ask if they will reduce your interest rate. The credit-card market is very competitive, so it is common that they will negotiate with you to keep your business.

e. If you are unable to pay your creditors the minimum due each month, organize your payments and give proportionately (pro rata) to each creditor his/her share of your total debt. Write each creditor and explain to them what you are about to do and send them a check attached to a copy of your budget and pro rata sheet. (There is a sample pro-rata sheet in the "Application" section of this chapter to illustrate this concept.)

NOTES

The Pro Rata Formula:

Creditor   Total Payoff / Total debt = Percent x Disposable income = New Pmt.
_____ $_____ / $_____ = ____% x $_____ = $_____

A Bit About Credit Cards

There are some interesting (and staggering) statistics available about credit card debt. In today's society, it is very difficult to live without some use of credit. As we have already discussed, it is important to be very careful and intentional with your handling of credit and to keep your borrowing under control. However, in most cases, utilizing credit drains more money away from you than the actual value (purchase price) of the item purchased.

It's easy to lose control of your spending when you use credit cards because you see no cash pass from your hand, so you don't feel the pain of spending. Instead you feel glamorous and powerful, and you wind up buying "stuff" you would never buy if you were paying cash. This is where the "cash management system" in chapter three becomes a very practical option for maintaining your budget.

"Plastic Surgery" makes sense!
- 78% of people don't pay off their credit card each month, even with planning.
- The average annual interest rate on credit cards is about 18%.
- 72 % of credit cards have variable rates (meaning your debts will go up if the rates do, and the new rates apply to the entire balance).
- The average credit card balance is $1950.
- Consumers spend 12% more on "general" purchases using credit, than they

NOTES

would if they used cash for the same purchases.
- Consumers spend 54% more on food (eating out/groceries) using credit than they would if they used cash.
- Most people spend less when paying with cash than when paying with a credit card.[1]

Finding low-interest credit cards

If you feel you are paying a higher interest rate on your credit card balance than necessary, you may need to shop around. Low-interest balance transfer offers (or introductory rates) are frequently available from credit card companies who want your business. This low-interest option can provide a way for you to pay down your principal balance faster. Be careful, though, this is only a good choice when you are no longer spending on credit cards, and if the credit card offers good terms when the balance transfer period ends.

Searching the Internet for credit cards is an easy way to find a lot of options in one place. Here are some things to consider when you are looking for a lower-interest credit card.
- Introductory Offer Period – some companies offer 0%, 2.9%, etc, for up to 12 months. Obviously, the longer that you can keep the low interest the better.
- Grace Period – look for cards that offer a grace period (typically 20 to 25 days). If there is no grace period, then you are accruing interest on your purchases immediately. This provides no opportunity to avoid an interest charge.
- Annual Fees – there are credit card companies that offer no annual fee. If

---

[1] The Financial Peace Planner, by Dave Ramsey, Penguin Books, 1998, page 101

NOTES

your current card carries an annual fee, it is not uncommon for them to waive it if you will ask. Annual fees can range from $25 to over $100 per year.

- Interest Rate Benchmark – after the introductory period (if there is one on the card that you select) the interest rate is usually pegged to a percentage over some published interest rate — usually prime rate. There is a wide variety in this category. Remember, if you can't pay your credit card balance off within the time frame of the introductory period, then the benchmark for the interest rate is a very important factor in your decision. This is how you will avoid paying over 20% on your credit card balance.

2. Go on a cash basis for every other purchase from this point forward. This will take commitment and accountability. Setting up and following a budget will assist in this process.

3. Consolidate debt with a bank loan or a debt-consolidation company. It may be reasonable to consider obtaining a loan to consolidate all of your consumer debt. Generally speaking, the interest on the loan will be less than the interest paid on consumer debt. Sometimes you can structure the loan so that you can make the maximum monthly payment to reduce the debt as rapidly as possible.

Another option might be a home equity loan. Because a home equity loan is considered a second mortgage and is tied to the value/equity of your home, you'll likely pay a lower interest rate. Beware of home-equity loans that offer more than 100 percent loan-to-value. Remember, if you borrow more than the value of the underlying asset, you are in debt. Another important factor to consider with a home-equity loan is that, if and when you sell your home, you

---

NOTES

are required to pay off the unpaid balance. Therefore, plan to accelerate home equity loan payments.

Two words of caution: 1) don't borrow against your house until — and only until — you have taken the painful steps to cut back and live within your means. Otherwise you are just borrowing from a different source to keep spending; and 2) if you don't pay cash for all future purchases once you have consolidated your debt, you'll end up back in the same hole that you were in before, and this time you'll have the consolidation loan on top of the consumer and credit card debt.

4. Know your borrowing power. Another key to debt management is to know how much you can reasonably expect to borrow. Borrowing power can be calculated by recognizing the amount of security you have in assets and the amount of cash flow that you can manage for debt retirement. As discussed in Chapter Three (Budgeting), the maximum that you should spend for debt service is 20% of your take-home pay after taxes, tithe, long-term savings, and other faith promise commitments. These figures do not include house payments. Based upon that figure, you can easily calculate the maximum amount that you can "afford" to borrow. (For additional help refer to the Household Budget Worksheet in chapter three.)

For example: Fred and Alice have a gross monthly paycheck of $4,600. After taxes, tithes, & retirement savings, their net income is $3225 per month. Using the 20% debt-service rule, they can "afford" $645 in monthly payments toward debt (credit cards, auto payments, and other loans). So, when they are deciding to finance their next vehicle or buy that furniture on credit, they will have a clearly established target for what they should plan to spend.

NOTES

Teaching Children About Debt

In chapter one I mentioned a statistic about college students with credit card debt. It was astounding to me how quickly and easily college kids can get into consumer debt. That same article described that the weight of the credit card payments pressures some students to cut back on their class schedules to earn more money at their part-time jobs or even to take a semester or a year off to catch up on their debt. How do they fall prey to this lie so easily? Well, access is one issue. Credit card companies make it so easy to obtain credit on campus. Another, deeper, reason however is that children and parents don't talk about debt in much detail prior to children going off to college. It is critical to set limits for any credit that the child will obtain and to discuss who will be paying the bills. The credit card companies are counting on parents to step up and pay down the balance, but this is not an appropriate arrangement for the student in most cases. Handling debt should be part of the child's educational process while they are still at home so that they will know how to handle the peer pressure of obtaining and using "plastic" when they go out on their own.

Practical Steps to Getting Out of Debt.[1]

1. Ask God for help. A first step in getting control of your finances is to ask God to give you new insight and wisdom about money matters. Jesus had more to say about money than he did almost any other subject. He knew that how we handle money has a lot to say about our inner spiritual life. So you can be assured he wants to help you overcome financial bondage. Ask God to give you

---

[1] Some of these tips were gleaned from Newsweek Magazine, August 27, 2001 issue, "Don't Lose It: Seven Tips," by Jane Bryant Quinn, page 38

NOTES

new resolve to be a wise and prudent steward over the resources he has entrusted to you.

2.   Write out a budget. A budget is a financial plan — a sort of financial map that will guide you out of financial bondage and into financial freedom. By making a budget, you can clearly see how much you have to spend for each category every month, and you can visualize how you can get from where you are now to where you need to be. Then use your budget religiously to keep track of spending.

3.   List all your debts and the interest you are paying on each one (with the aid of a discerning friend or spouse). Use the "My Present Debt Load" worksheet to make a debt-retirement plan, and then follow through. Take any windfall money or spare dollars and pay down debt. Take your income tax return and before even thinking about how you can spend it, send it to Visa or MasterCard to pay down your credit card debt. Paying off the small balances first will be an immediately tangible reward.

4.   Get outside assistance. Ask your pastor or an elder in your church if there is someone in your church body that can mentor you and teach you about finances. Most churches have people who have a good handle on financial matters. Some of them work in the financial industry. By yourself you may not have the knowledge or commitment to change your borrowing habits. Let them teach and advise you about what steps you should take to go from financial bondage to financial freedom.

NOTES

5. Practice full disclosure. If you are married, commit to tell each other about how you are individually spending money. Often couples with separate checking accounts don't know how the other marriage partner is spending money. All too often they don't want their spouse to know.

6. Deprive yourself. Stop spending for things you can do without. Agree with your spouse that you will not make any major consumer purchases (furniture, appliances, stereos, cars, expensive vacations, etc.) for at least two years.

7. Become content with what you have. Credit cards don't sneak out of our wallet or purse in the middle of the night and go on a spending spree all by themselves. Credit card debt is the result of you (and your spouse if married) spending money you really don't have. It would be one thing if it were spent on emergency medical necessities or some other "must-have" item. But most credit card debt is accumulated from buying things we really don't need. They are impulse "wants," not necessities. Remember that how you spend your money shows where your priorities lie. Jesus said, "Where your treasure is, there will your heart be also." (Matt. 6:20, 21) "The choice isn't between saving (for college) and a 401(k), it's between saving and leasing a BMW," says financial planner Paul White of Manassas, Virginia. Until you face the real problem and decide to change your behavior, there isn't any financial plan that can help you.

8. Consider using a debit card. This gives the convenience of a credit card, but takes the funds directly from your checking account. Keep track of these purchases in your checkbook register to avoid overdraws on your account.

NOTES

9.   Consider discontinuing contributions to savings or retirement plans. Do this until your debt is paid off. It doesn't make sense to receive 7% on your investments if you are paying 18% on debts.

10. Live on less than you earn each month. Then take the balance and begin to repay debt and start a savings account. Your immediate reaction might be that there is no way to cut spending. But almost always there are things you can find to cut, which we discussed in chapter four (Spending). If you are living above your means, scale back. Turn your attention to building relationships, not buying more.

11. Keep track of the cash you get from ATMs. Cash isn't called "liquid" by accident. If you don't keep track, it will go right through your fingers. Use the cash management worksheets in the budgeting chapter to help you keep track.

12. Discontinue any purchases which are not absolutely essential, especially services that you can perform for yourself. Also, sell any items which have high depreciating rates, such as a new car or a new major appliance, and replace them, if necessary, with similar items that have lower depreciating rates like a used car or a used appliance.

13. Reduce your credit card collection to one card. The average couple has seven or eight credit cards, often charging on one to make a payment on another. Consumer credit companies don't care if you're "dog paddling" in debt. They want you to build up as much debt as possible so that they can earn more and more interest. Get an all-purpose card like a MasterCard, VISA, or Discover.

NOTES

Choose one with the lowest interest rate you can find. This card then becomes the card that you will use for check writing identification, car rental, and genuine "stuck out in the boonies" emergencies—things you must use a credit card for. If you must have a credit card for business travel, make a vow that you will only spend on legitimate business travel that is either deductible or reimbursable by your company. Stop using credit cards for everything else. It is a proven fact that people spend less when they use cash. You will be amazed how you can adapt to life post-plastic!

14. Start a crisis fund. On a regular basis, put away money (however small) for emergencies. Then vow only to use that money for true emergencies. Medical emergencies, appliance breakdowns (such as water heaters or furnaces, but not such things as stereos or TVs) qualify as emergencies; a huge sale at Nordstrom's does not.

15. Give God a chance to provide an item before you buy it. There is no rule that says you can't pray for the specific item that you need, and trust that God will provide it in a miraculous way. Don't presume on faith by making a large purchase and then asking God to send you the money to pay for it.

16. Ask these questions before borrowing:
- Have I prayed about borrowing for this item?
- Am I getting something of value that is worth the added obligation?
- Will the asset purchased appreciate in value?
- Will the borrowing allow me to give, save, and maintain my lifestyle?
- Does the borrowing fit my budget?

NOTES

- Will the borrowing cause any tension or anxiety in my family?
- Is my borrowing showing any unhealthy pattern?

Start Today!

Other than your home mortgage and perhaps a car loan, your goal should be to eliminate all consumer debt so that you can use the money you have for saving and investing in your future and the future of your family and ministry. From this day forward, make a decision to cease robbing your future to pay for the past. Make the decision that today you will pay on a cash basis. You will purchase those things that must be purchased with cash, or you will wait. The most important decision you can make is to think debt free and be debt free.

NOTES

For Application

Personal Finance Improvement Checklist

____ Review the "Practical Steps to Getting out of Debt" and see which ones you are not currently practicing. Determine, with the help of God, to put all of these steps into practice. Write down some goals and steps you need to take to get from where you are now to where you need to be.

____ Consider your current debts by completing the "My Present Debt Load" worksheet and develop a plan to pay off all consumer debt early. If needed, consult with a trusted advisor on how to do this.

____ Sell any unnecessary high depreciation assets and use the proceeds to pa off debt?

____ Evaluate your debt and determine which is debt as defined in the chapter and which is not debt. Have you ever thought of your financial position in this way?

____ Read through the concepts in this section regarding methods for auto purchases and mortgage reduction. Are there suggestions there that you can implement now or work toward in the future? What are they?

_____

_____

_____

____ Check into your options for refinancing high interest debts, including credit cards, home and personal loans.

____ Research credit card companies to find the best program for your situation.

____ If you are married, discuss these things with your spouse.

____ Determine a future when you plan to be out of debt and work toward that goal.

____ If needed, cut up all of your credit cards and begin using the cash management system.

My Present Debt Load Worksheet

To get out of debt, you first need to understand how much debt you owe. Fill out this worksheet to gain a clear picture of your situation. You may need to call your lenders to find the most current figures and ask if they will lower your rates. If you are currently making extra payments, please list them. If you can make extra payments to one or more creditors, decide how much, list it, and then circle that line.

Creditor	Present Balance	Min. Monthly Payment	Interest Rate	Lower Rate	Extra Payments
Mortgage	$ _____	$ _____	_____	_____	$ _____
2nd Mortgage	$ _____	$ _____	_____	_____	$ _____
Education	$ _____	$ _____	_____	_____	$ _____
Credit Card - _____	$ _____	$ _____	_____	_____	$ _____
Credit Card - _____	$ _____	$ _____	_____	_____	$ _____
Credit Card - _____	$ _____	$ _____	_____	_____	$ _____
Gas Card - _____	$ _____	$ _____	_____	_____	$ _____
Car Loan - _____	$ _____	$ _____	_____	_____	$ _____
Loan - _____	$ _____	$ _____	_____	_____	$ _____
Loan - _____	$ _____	$ _____	_____	_____	$ _____
Loan - _____	$ _____	$ _____	_____	_____	$ _____
Doctor - _____	$ _____	$ _____	_____	_____	$ _____
Other - _____	$ _____	$ _____	_____	_____	$ _____
Other - _____	$ _____	$ _____	_____	_____	$ _____
Totals	$ _____	$ _____			$ _____

Pay More Than the Minimum!

This chart points out the major difference in the interest expense and the number of payments at different monthly payments. The typical credit card company requires a minimum payment of 1.5% of the outstanding balance, which would be $45.00 in our example of a $3,000 balance. Note also the major expense in the Interest Paid column when the interest rate is at 18% versus at ten percent. This information should be incentive to pay more than the minimum and search for the lowest interest rate card that you can find!

Credit Balance	Percentage Rate	Monthly Pymt	Interest Paid	No.of Pymts.
$3000	10%	$45.00	$1,397	98
		$60.00	$ 896	65
		$90.00	$ 529	40
$3000	14%	$45.00	$2,835	130
		$60.00	$1,528	76
		$90.00	$ 821	43
$3000	18%	$45.00	$8,830	258
		$60.00	$2,587	94
		$90.00	$1,189	47

Sample Pro-Rata Worksheet:

This example is designed for those who are unable to pay even the minimum on each of their credit accounts. The primary issue is to communicate openly and honestly with your creditors. This worksheet can demonstrate to them that you want to meet your financial commitments and that you have a plan to do so.

To use the pro-rata formula, you first need to determine the total monthly payment you can apply to your credit cards (including furniture and appliance accounts). This is the figure that you will then divide among the various creditors based on their percentage of your total debt.

In this example, the total debt is $7,800 and monthly minimum payments total $234. Our individual has only $150.00 available per month to pay toward these bills.

	Acct. Bal.	Min. Mo. Pymt.	Acct. bal, as % of total debt	New Pymt. Amt.
Card 1	$2,000	$60.00	$2000/7800 = 26%	$150 x 26% = $39.00
Card 2	$1,500	$45.00	$1500/7800 = 19%	$150 x 19% = $28.50
Card 3	$ 500	$15.00	$500/7800 = 6%	$150 x 6% = $ 9.00
Card 4	$3,800	$114.00	$3800/7800 = 49%	$150 x 49% = $73.50

This chart should accompany a letter of explanation of your payment plan and goals as well as a check in the amount of the suggested payment. Essentially, you are proposing to pay your creditors an amount equal to their percentage of your total debt. This should sound better to them than receiving no payment at all.

Calculating Your Personal Debt Reduction Plan

- Extra payment margin (usually 10% - 15% of your monthly take home pay) $_____.
- Write down each debt account in column A.
- Write down current balance in column B.
- Write down regular monthly payment in column C.
- Divide column B by column C and put the answer in column D.
- Sort, arranging from the shortest duration to the longest duration. (Number from 1 to the end of the list) put in column E.
- Take the dollars allocated to the extra payment margin (#1 above) and spread it among the accounts to shorten the duration to pay-off beginning with the highest number in column E. Place the actual dollars in Column F.
- Calculate the effect of these additional funds on the duration of full pay-off by adding F to C and dividing B by C.

I. Account II. Name (A)	Current Balance (B)	Monthly Pymt (C)	Mos. to Pay (B divided by C) (D)	Sort Shortest to longest (E)	Added Payment Plan (F)	Planned Months to Payoff (G)
1.						
2.						
3.						
4.						
5.						
6.						

Save on Car Purchases

For most Americans their car is the second largest purchase they make, but it occurs much more often than buying a house. The average couple will purchase 10 to 12 vehicles between the ages of 30 and 65. If purchased wisely, there is no reason why you can't save tens of thousands of dollars on auto purchases in your lifetime, leaving more money for you to save and invest.

Tips to help you:

1. Never borrow on a depreciating asset, unless you have enough down payment and short terms. Borrow three years or less on a car because its value typically drops faster than the loan balance after three years.

2. Leasing is the most expensive way to go. Dealers push leasing because they make big money by leasing. By leasing you pay a lot of money every month to not own anything at the end of your term.

3. If you insist on buying new:
- Consider a year-end model, when dealers offer added buying incentives.
- Compare dealer costs by checking newspaper and website ads and pricing.
- Research the retail/wholesale/invoice prices in NADA and Kelly Blue Book.
- Buy at month's end when dealers are highly motivated to meet selling quotas.
- Make sure you know how much you can borrow by getting pre-qualified.
- Check insurance rates for models you are considering buying.
- Make at least a 25% down payment and payments as large as you can afford.
- Negotiate price, and buy a car based upon total price, not the size of the payment.
- Never purchase expensive disability or credit life insurance from auto dealers.
- Learn how to say "no" to a car dealer. As the buyer you are in the "driver's seat!"
- If you have a "trade-in", sell it yourself and get 20-25% more for it than a dealer will give you for it as a trade-in. You lose your negotiating power when you trade-in.

4. **If you are content with buying used:**
   - Buy a car that is 2-4 years old, has low mileage, and in good condition.
   - Consider lease/rental return vehicles that have been well maintained.
   - Buy vehicles with a potentially higher resale value.

5. **Buy your car with cash:**
   The main reason people spend more than they can afford on car is that they finance it. To eliminate the 10-30% you pay on loan interest try this: Once you have paid off your current car loan, set aside the payment amount in a high interest bearing account and save up for your next car purchase.

Options for paying off your home mortgage early

1. **Make additional payments.** You may be able to save thousands of dollars off your mortgage debt by making extra payments. Using the mortgage scenario #1 below and paying an extra $50 more each month you would save $35,293 in interest and reduce your payments by 7.2 years. Paying an extra $100 per month would save you $53,757 in interest and cut 11.1 years off your loan. This is an ideal option if: a) you have a high interest rate loan; b) still have plenty of years left on your loan; c) want the assurance that your loan will be paid off in a pre-determined time frame.

2. **Arrange a personal "Mortgage Reduction Account."** If you prefer to personally invest monies used for extra mortgage payments, this may be an option for you. Rather than sending extra payments to your lender, you can invest them in a growth fund until they equal your mortgage balance and use them to pay off your balance in one lump sum. The advantages of this strategy are that you are in full control of the assets and have the ability to use some or all of the monies for emergencies or other purposes.

3. **Make bi-weekly payments.** Some lenders allow you to make a mortgage payment every two weeks rather than paying once per month. If you are able to do this, it is the equivalent of making an extra payment each year. The result is a significant interest savings and having your mortgage paid off seven to eight years earlier.

MORTGAGE SCENARIO #1:

Borrow $80,000 for 30 years at 7.75% interest

Principal and interest payments for 30 years would be: $206,327

The minimum monthly principal & interest payments: $573.13

Total principal paid: $80,000

Total interest paid: $126,327

MORTGAGE SCENARIO #2:

Borrow $80,000 for 15 years at 7.25% interest

(shorter term mortgages usually carry a lower interest rate)

Principal and interest payments for 15 years would be: $131,452

The minimum monthly principal & interest payments: $730.29

Total principal paid: $80,000

Total interest paid: $51,452

Interest savings over the 30-year, 7.75% loan in scenario #1: $74,875

If you can afford the higher loan payments, this is a great savings options!

NOTES

Reflections on Debt Management

1. Debt is bondage according to **Proverbs 22:26-27**. The reasons that we get into debt are numerous, one of which is Desire as described in the chapter. **Read Proverbs 23:1-5 and 19-21** and identify the folly of striving for the things that others have. Which reason(s) for getting into debt did you relate to in the chapter?

    _____

    _____

    _____

2. Does getting out of debt feel impossible to you? **Read the story of the widow's oil in II Kings 4:17.** What was the key to God's miraculous provision for the widow and her sons? The widow was obedient even though what she was told to do seemed impossible. Do you believe that God can help you get out of debt and provide for your needs in the process? Is He instructing you today to trust Him and to take action to begin paying off your debt even though it seems to be impossible? Give serious consideration to your answer and write your thoughts below.

    _____

    _____

    _____

3. **Read Psalm 37: 3-5** and reflect on your responses above and on the things that you learned in the chapter. Make a vow before God not to incur more debt while paying off the debt you now have and trust Him to help you.

4. Additional Scriptures for review and reflection:
    Psalm 118:8, Luke 16:10-12, Romans 13:7-9

Prayer: *Lord, I confess that my misguided motives and attitudes have caused me to fall into the bondage of too much debt. Please change my heart so that my attitude will be one of contentment for the things that I already have, and give me a constant motivation to stick to my debt reduction strategies. Help me to trust in your provision and to be obedient like the widow in II Kings, even though it seems like an impossible achievement to me just now.*

CHAPTER 6

Saving

Consistently Save and Invest with a Purpose

In chapter three (Budgeting), I suggested a target for savings of 10% of your net income. In this chapter, we'll discuss the various reasons to save, and the types of savings vehicles available depending on the purpose for the funds. For our purposes in this chapter, the terms saving and investing will be used interchangeably, with both terms meaning an amount of money set aside for a future purpose.

The amount of money you spend to care for your family's needs will determine how much you can invest. As we discussed in the last couple of chapters, overspending robs God and limits future investment opportunities.

> *"...a foolish man devours all he has."*
>
> Proverbs 21:20

An important biblical concept of stewardship places a great deal of responsibility upon us for taking care of our family by properly managing the assets entrusted to us by God. The parable of the talents in Matthew 25:14-30 shows us that God wants us to multiply the money He gives us, no matter how large or small the amount. However, God gives you and me the freedom to choose what to do with that money. Your individual circumstances will determine the type of investments that are favorable for you.

For some people the habit of saving on a consistent basis is a piece of cake. It seems to just be a natural part of their nature. For the rest of us, howev-

---

NOTES

er, it is not an automatic part of our makeup and is a discipline that needs to be developed over time. As with most disciplines in life, the hardest part is to just get started. My friend, Debbie, the youth pastor mentioned in an earlier chapter, shares a story from her life that illustrates this point of developing a habit of savings very well.

Finances were a challenge most of the time in my first ministry after college. But from the start, when I was planning my budget before getting that first paycheck, I decided to build a habit of saving into my life. I didn't have much to live on, let alone save, but I designated $5 each month for savings. It was a laughable amount, but nonetheless served to help me form a lifetime habit of saving. As my income grew, so did the amount of my monthly savings. This habit allowed me to pay semi-annual bills up front, take some vacations, pay for half of my wedding, and be a stay-at-home wife for a while after the wedding, besides keeping my "financial" house in order.

The two key points to take from this story are 1) start developing the mindset and the habit of savings, and 2) it doesn't matter the amount, because it is the habit that really counts.

Believe it or not, it is possible to live within or below your means in today's society so that you can put money aside for the future and still have a fulfilling life. Society pressures us into thinking just the opposite — that we are somehow deprived if we don't accumulate all of the "trappings" that their definition of success requires. Dave Gerig, who collaborated with me on this book, shares the story of his financial journey through 20+ years of marriage. He and

NOTES

his wife were diligent and thoughtful in their financial planning from the beginning. You will see how this method of financial management, called delayed gratification, pays off in more than just money in the bank. Despite some periodic financial setbacks over the years, they have experienced a peace of mind, contentment, and a lack of marital strain due to financial issues.

I learned the value of saving and investing early in life and married a woman who has a similar attitude about financial stewardship, especially in the areas of spending and saving money. We started our life together with a joint resolve to be frugal, economy-minded, debt free, and able to handle money God's way. It has paid off in many ways.

Diane and I set a goal of owning a home within 3-5 years. I was a part-time college ministries pastor and operated a part-time floor covering business out of our home, while Diane worked full-time. We established some spending restraints, as well as guidelines for saving and investing. We developed a budget and stuck to it, including putting 15% toward savings. It wasn't easy and we had to make constant adjustments, but we stuck to our budget and established some healthy habits.

Rather than trying to amass in a few years the kind of possessions that it took our parents 25-30 years to purchase we resolved to stick to our budget. Our first apartment living room was furnished and decorated modestly with a combination of used, hand-made, and inexpensive items. We chose to own good used cars, eat the majority of our meals at home (Diane is great cook!), and not splurge on clothes or gifts, so that we would not be burdened with debt and put our future goals out of reach.

While pursuing the goal of purchasing our first home, we experienced a

NOTES

few challenges and setbacks. I decided to earn a master's degree in counseling, so we faced large tuition bills and temporarily reduced our savings. Our first child was born at the beginning of our fifth year of marriage and Diane was off work for many months. With only one income we had to alter our lifestyle in order to continue regular savings of any kind. Then we moved to Northern California where the cost of living increased dramatically. We struggled to remain disciplined savers, but never lost sight of our goal. We read a couple of books on personal money management and learned some basic spending and saving tactics. Plus, I taught stewardship principles to couples, reaping the benefits of practicing what I preached.

When we couldn't pay cash for an item or a vacation with our savings then we simply wouldn't buy it. We also had an agreement to consult with one another before making purchases over $20. We learned that to reach our financial goals we had to say "no" to many little things in the present in order to say "yes" to more important things in the future. When more expensive items were on our "wish list" we researched the product, shopped around, prayed about it and waited 24 hours after determining the best option. In most cases we decided that the item was not actually a need and chose not to make the purchase. Instead, we put the funds we would have spent into a savings account.

We were able to save in excess of $20,000 over the first seven years of our marriage, and were easily able to purchase our first home in the Seattle area. It took seven years to buy that home instead of five, but we did it!

Since then we have diligently saved for vacations, cars, and furniture (for which we paid cash), and put away funds for retirement and college tuition for our two children. Over the years we felt some pressure from our family,

---

NOTES

friends and society who encouraged us to purchase things they considered to be "needs," but we saw as "wants." We're glad we remained committed to "delayed gratification." We learned to put our trust in God, pray for direction, commit our financial plans to Him, be sensitive to the leading of the Holy Spirit, honor God with His tithe and our offerings, and have experienced many blessings from God's hand. Every person's story will be different, but when we understand that the Lord is the source and owner of everything, and faithfully honor God by following His plans, we can live a rich and contented life without the burden of debt and financial bondage.

Reasons to Save

It's one thing to suggest a savings target, but what are we supposed to do with that 10%? Below are four simple reasons to save at least 10% of your income:

1. Save to build an emergency fund (equivalent of 3 months of income).
2. Save for major purchases to avoid debt (water heater, automobile repairs, home entertainment system, vacation, etc.). Note: Auto repairs, including tire purchases, are paid for on credit a majority of the time. This is an area that people tend to overlook when planning their auto expenses.
3. Save for future needs and giving (missionaries, charitable gifts, friends in need, etc.).
4. Save for retirement.

In chapter five (Debt Management) Fred and Alice used the 70/20/10 budget maintenance formula to determine how much they could afford in monthly payments toward debt. Using their same net income as an example ($3225 per

NOTES

month after taxes, tithes, & retirement savings), they should be putting at least $322.50 per month into a savings account. Now they need to decide what is an appropriate amount to put toward each of the four categories that we just listed above? This is where it is helpful to know your investment objectives.

Investment Objectives

Many people have no idea where to invest their money or really how to start. In fact, the word "invest" is more intimidating than the word "save." So many people still believe that "investing" is for the wealthy, when in reality it is something that applies to anyone who is planning for their financial futures. A good starting place is to picture yourself where you want to be 5, 10, or 20 years from now. After you've set your goals, you are in a position to develop a plan to get there (refer to the goal setting and net worth worksheets in chapter 3). Savvy investors select a mix of savings and investment vehicles in order to meet their variety of objectives.

"The servant with two-thousand showed how he also had doubled his masters investment. His master commended him: 'Good work! You did your job well. From now on be my partner.'"
Matthew 25:22-23
(The Message)

Depending on your short-term and long-term goals for your savings, you will choose different investment vehicles to reach those goals. Obviously, if you are putting a portion of your savings away for college tuition, you will not (or should not) select a bank savings account that is earning 2% or less and allows extremely easy access to the funds. For most of us, this kind of access offers too great a temptation to draw the funds for some "great deal" on a vacation, sound system, or other major purchase with the good intention of paying it

NOTES

back later. It is a better plan to tie those education savings funds up in a long-term vehicle with restricted access and higher interest earnings, thus limiting your temptation to use the funds to true emergency purposes only. On the other hand, if a portion of your 10% savings allocation is for auto repairs or other emergency needs, then you will want to find an account that does not restrict access. Here is what Fred and Alice are doing with their 10% savings funds of $322.50 each month:

Fund Purpose	Emergency	Auto Repairs/Main. & Maintenance	Vacation/Fun Fund & Christmas Fund	Tuition
Amount Saved	$100 per month = $1,200 per year	$25 per month = $300 per year	$100 per month = $1200 per year	$100 per month = $1200 per year
Savings Vehicle	Interest-bearing savings acct.	Interest-bearing savings acct.	6 mo. bank CD or equivalent int. bearing savings acct.	Education IRA

Start Now!

Remember Debbie's story of putting only $5 per month into savings? Well, even though she said that it was a "laughable amount," the chart below shows how a little can go a long way when you are consistent. As you implement a saving strategy and put those funds into an interest-bearing account, look at the benefits that you will reap for years to come.

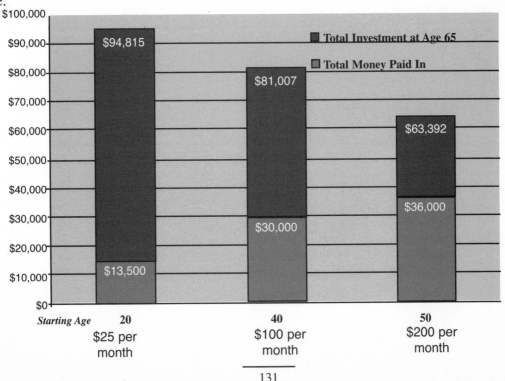

This chart demonstrates the powerful practice of saving over time.

1. If you started saving $25 per month in an account that earns 7% at the age of 20 until age 65, you would put in only $13,500 over that period of years, but your account would equal $94,815 — nearly $100,000!

2. If you wait for 20 years, and try to make up the lost time by saving four times that amount, you will put in $30,000 by the age of 65 and only have $81,007.

3. Now, wait ten more years and start saving $200 per month at the age of 50 and you have lost a lot of financial opportunity. You would put $36,000 into your account and achieve only $63,392.

So, you see, the saying that "Time is Money" is true in this context. Whether you have $5.00 per month or $500 per month to save, I encourage you to develop your savings goals and start today! The longer that you wait, the more difficult it may be to catch up!

If you are already in the habit of saving, but this chapter has given your habit some purpose and focus, then our work on this topic is done! However, if you are struggling to create the habit of saving, you may have dealt with some feelings of frustration with yourself because of the lack of discipline. For you, I have some suggestions to help you develop a habit of saving.

1. Save money from every paycheck and put it in an interest earning account.

2. Use automatic withdrawal or electronic funds transfer (EFT) from your

---

NOTES

checking account into your savings vehicle if it is available to you. EFT is a great way to start the discipline of saving because it happens automatically and you don't have to struggle to remember to write the check each time.

3. Put a portion of your funds in an account with easy access so you can get to it if and when you need it. The following list of vehicles would work well for a short-term emergency fund or major-purchase savings fund:
    a. Savings accounts — Savings and Loans, Banks and Credit Unions
    b. Certificates of Deposit — Insured time deposits
    c. Money Market Funds — Mutual funds with a variety of short-term indebtedness, like T-bills, CDs, etc.

4. Write your savings account a check just as if it were a creditor.

5. Any time an existing debt is paid off, reallocate that money to your savings plan.

The Miracle of Compound Interest

In the previous savings graph, the example is based on 7% interest, compounded monthly. Compounding interest is a powerful investment concept that helps your money to earn money. A common rule of thumb for evaluating the success of an investment is how long it takes for the initial principal amount to double. A shorthand method for calculating the doubling rate is called the "Rule of 72":

(72) divided by (the interest rate earned) = the number of years to double your money.

NOTES

The chart below reflects the doubling rate at a range of interest rates:

Rate of Return:	4%	5%	6%	7%	8%	10%	12%	14%	20%
Years to Double:	18	14	12	10	9	7.2	6	5	3.6

When you plan to save for the long term (i.e. retirement, real estate investments, college tuition, etc.), investing at a high rate of return is the smartest move. The example below is a clear picture of the power of compounding interest at higher rates.

$1,000 one time investment - no withdrawals - from age 25 to age 65
6% interest   = $10,957
12% interest   = $118,648
18% interest   = $1,269,698

In fact, just two-percentage points difference makes a great impact:

	10 years	20 years	30 years
10% return	$2,707	$7,328	$19,837
12% return	$3,300	$10,893	$35,950

Don't wait until you have "enough money" to justify savings. Starting as early as possible with even a little is a smarter idea than waiting until you have achieved an income level that allows you to save a lot.

NOTES

Understand Investment Risk

Today's investment options are vast. The lower the risk of losing your principal, the lower the potential rate of return. Investments that have the potential for huge gains and big profits also carry a substantial risk of loss. But in investing, risk comes in many shapes and sizes. Some risks are quite obvious, while others are less obvious. The investment company, Dain Rauscher (www.dainrauscher.com), cites some risks that are often overlooked.

The risk of not investing. Believe it or not, the biggest risk to your financial security is to do nothing. It's the same with your body. While exercise has the potential to hurt you, sitting still just isn't a healthy alternative.

The risk of playing it too safe. Another odd one. But it's possible that investors who refuse to assume some level of risk can lose in the long run. If, for example, you saved money diligently all your working years but insisted on investing in CDs, your savings may not have grown enough to surpass inflation and meet your needs.

"Take the thousand and give it to the one who risked the most. And get rid of this 'play-it-safe' who won't go out on a limb."
Matthew 25:28-29
(The Message)

The risk of not planning ahead. Perhaps you invest faithfully for years, enjoying good returns from your investments. But when you stop to calculate your expenses, you find that you haven't been saving enough money to realistically meet your financial goals.

The risk of extremes. Investors who refuse to diversify are taking a gamble,

---

NOTES

regardless of in what basket they're putting their eggs. It's a careful balance, however, because too much diversification can also be risky. When investors chase varying products from year to year, their investment portfolios become a crazy quilt of holdings with no particular pattern. The risk here is usually under performance, though most anything is possible.

The risk of solid investment. Solid investments are good, but if they're not liquid, you might end up in hot water. If you put your all money in conservative investments such as CDs, and you suddenly need or want your cash back, you may trade your gains for prepayment penalties.

Strategies to Reduce Risk

Diversify. Most types of risk can be managed by diversification dividing investment dollars among different industries, countries, and asset classes (stocks, bonds, real estate, etc.). "Spreading the risk" through diversification helps cushion the impact that problems in one investment might have on a portfolio. Mutual Funds are a popular investment vehicle, partly because they enable investors to instantly diversify.

Be patient. Invest for the long term to reduce risk. Very high stock-market returns occur only over short periods. On the other hand, losses disappear almost completely over ten-year holding periods, and they vanish over a twenty-year time frame.

Jump in gradually. Lump sum investing can produce spectacular returns if your timing is right. That's a big "if." Very few professional investors con-

---

NOTES

sistently "time" the market correctly, and individual investors are notorious for timing it incorrectly, buying at market tops and selling at market bottoms. For most investors, dollar-cost averaging investing a fixed amount of money on a monthly basis provides a disciplined approach that can reduce investment risks and improve long-term returns.

Where you choose to put your money reflects the investment strategy you're using. In grandpa's day, the family savings were often tucked under a mattress, hidden in the flour bowl, or stuffed in a hole in the wall. The following investment approaches represent various degrees of risk versus reward.

1. *Conservative Risk*: Investments in T-bonds and bills, money market funds, bank CDs, and other fixed-income investments. Low-risk investments, such as bonds, increase the chances of getting your money back plus interest.

2. *Limited Risk*: Blue-chip stocks, high-rated corporate bonds, high-rated municipal bonds, income mutual funds.

3. *Moderate Risk*: Growth stocks, mutual funds, low-rated corporate bonds, growth mutual funds, large-cap stocks, and some blue-chip stocks.

4. *Speculative Risk*: Speculative stocks, futures, high-yield bonds, and international investments with major risk and unpredictable results.

NOTES

Guidelines for Determining Risk Tolerance

You may be asking the question, "How do I determine the difference between an okay and a foolish investment risk? Here are five rules that you can apply to make this decision:

1. If you can't afford to lose it, you shouldn't risk it.
2. If taking a particular risk will cause you to lose sleep, you should look elsewhere. Everyone must pass the investment "sleep test."
3. If you don't obtain counsel from one or more investment counselors who have more wisdom and experience than you before making a questionable investment, you may in for a rude awakening.
4. If your motive for taking a risk to multiply your assets is based upon greed, it's wrong! "If you already have enough, there's no reason to risk it all on the possibility of earning more." (Larry Burkett – The World's Easiest Guide to Finances - page 150)
5. Pray and ask the Lord for direction and a "peace" before launching out, rather than asking Him to bless an unsure move after-the-fact.

Take the quiz at the end of the chapter to determine your risk tolerance.

Investment Asset Allocations

Once you have two nickels to rub together, it's a good idea to keep them in separate pockets -- and not in the same pair of pants. The way you divide your money among different investment choices that suit your goals, time frame, and risk tolerance is called allocation. it is wise to diversify using some growth investments (large-, mid- and small-cap stocks and foreign stocks), long, medium

---

NOTES

and short-term bonds, income funds, fixed-income investments (CDs and money market funds), and possibly real estate. Having a mix of assets is excellent protection against drastic negative swings in one investment class or sector (like what occurred in the stock market in 2000). The process of building an asset allocation plan involves wise judgment and there are no textbook answers. The following chart is an example of asset allocations over a life span for someone with modest goals and a moderate risk tolerance.

Age	Life Cycle	Major Needs	Possible Allocation
20's	Complete education & beginning a family	Tuition, car, home, furnishings, financial protection	65% Growth Stocks 10% Muni Bonds 5% Income Fund 20% Money Market/CD
30/	Working family with younger children	Child expenses, reserve fund, retirement savings	55% Growth Stocks 15% Muni Bonds 15% Income Fund 15% Money Market/CDs
40s	Peak earner with older children	Retirement and college savings, home relocation, pay off debt, make a career change?	50% Growth Stocks 15% Muni Bonds 20% Income Fund 15% Money Market/CDs
50s	Empty nester and pre-retirement	College tuition, retirement savings, changing lifestyle, estate planning.	45% Growth Stocks 20% Muni Bonds 25% Income Fund 10% Money Market/CDs
60s+	Retirement	Changed lifestyle, volunteer service, travel, philanthropy	20% Growth Stocks 40% Muni Bonds 20% Income Fund 20% Money Market/CDs

NOTES

As Christians, in addition to God's call to be wise stewards of our resources through asset allocation, we have the added responsibility of not investing in companies that profit from ventures that are contrary to our morals. This is called "Moral Investing" or "Socially Responsible Investing" where organizations or funds are selected because they have products and services that either conform with or support values that the investor holds. Investment portfolios can be screened using criteria that are based on moral principles as a primary consideration to avoid companies that profit from abortion, pornography, immoral entertainment, tobacco, gambling, and alcohol. There is no guarantee that moral investment funds will outperform other investments, but research indicates that these funds have held their own over the past few years. If you are unaware of the business activities represented by the companies you have invested in, you may want to check them out. If you become uncomfortable with your investments from a moral perspective, remember that you have choices.

Common Mistakes to Avoid

Once you have evaluated your investment objectives, set financial goals, studied investment vehicles and financial concepts, evaluated strategies, risk tolerance, and asset allocations, it's time to implement your strategies. Now that you have some knowledge under your belt, you will want to be aware of a variety of mistakes that are commonly made.

1. Following the Crowd. The "herd instinct" means that you buy or sell when everyone else buys and sells. When you do this, you assume the crowd is right. This approach is primarily based on greed. Don't let the crowd determine your financial future.

NOTES

2. Avoiding Risk. If you are unwilling to take some risk, your investments will probably only keep pace with inflation. It's okay to take "calculated risks," but not "foolish risks." Get to know your risk tolerance level and seek advice from a professional to determine if your risk tolerance is appropriate to your investment objectives.

3. Acting on a "Hot Tip." The best investments result from careful analysis and hard work.

4. Not Monitoring Your Investment's Performance. Keeping good records is a must!

5. Not Following Through with Your Conviction to Save. If you don't save, you can't invest. Save consistently to achieve your goals.

6. Buying into a Financial Scam. People who are prone to believing all they hear (gullible) are prone to be misled and manipulated. They are easy targets for investment scams.

As you implement some of these strategies and your investments increase, you must be aware of your attitude. Be sure to never let your money begin to own you as it grows. Proverbs 11:28 says, *"Whoever trusts in his riches will fall, but the righteous will thrive like a green leaf."*

Strategically Plan for Your Retirement

People are living longer and retiring earlier these days. It used to be that people retired at 65 and most died by age 72. Today some of us will retire at 55

NOTES

or 60, and because of great medical advances, many of us will live to 85 or 90 or even longer. Instead of a few years of retirement, many people will experience 30 or more years of life after work.

Planning for retirement isn't something that you postpone until the year before you stop working.

Inadequately funding your retirement could lead to the following consequences:

- Keep you from fulfilling your dreams
- Plunge you into boredom and depression
- Force you to lower your standard of living
- Make you work longer than you had expected
- Reduce or eliminate your inheritance to family or ministry
- Not provide the freedom to serve the Lord as you would like

A Christian Perspective of Retirement

Most people believe that they can stop working at some point in their lives and enjoy a different lifestyle. How does that fit with being a Christian? Is retirement biblical? Scripture does not refer to retirement, so how should we apply this concept to our faith?

For Christians, retirement can be a time to:

- Volunteer in your church
- Help with a missions project
- Serve in your community, schools, etc.
- Remain active in your profession
- Begin a new career

NOTES

- Travel or pursue your hobbies

Retirement should be viewed as a slowing down rather than an end to your working years. However, upon retirement, if you use your extra money, time, and energy to simply eat, drink, and be merry, you are being a poor steward of God's gifts. According to the parable of the rich fool in Luke 12:13-21, those who store up things for themselves only and are not rich toward God are called "fools" and "will never get what they have prepared for themselves." Plus, as God's stewards we are blessed with the "fruit of the spirit" found in Galatians 5:22-23. By the time you are retired, this fruit has been developed and needs an outlet.

Planning a lazy and inactive retirement is not only discouraged by Scripture, it is also poses a risk to your health. Besides providing needed or extra income, a key by-product of working beyond retirement age is that you tend to live longer. A study at Harvard University certifies this fact. Their study looked at one hundred 65 year-old male grads that retired and 100 who had not. At age 75, seven out of eight of the retirees had died, while 7 out of 8 of the non-retirees were still alive and well. Some of the men who retired may have done so because of health reasons, but there are other explanations for the difference.[3] Does that mean that you have to work (employment in the traditional sense) until you're 75? Certainly not. The objective is to save enough during your working years so that you can use your retirement years to fulfill your God-given desires.

Everyone dreams of a rewarding and fulfilling retirement. Avoid these common planning pitfalls to achieve your goals.

- No goal setting

---

[3] Preparing for Retirement, by Larry Burkett, Moody Press, 1992, pg. 68

NOTES

- Lack of disciplined saving
- Inept and unwise investment strategies
- Poor tax planning
- Too much dependence on Social Security
- Retiring too early
- Not allowing for longer life expectancies
- Procrastination
- Inflation
- Inadequate financial planning

The whole concept of retirement is changing and for many of us retiring at age 65 is no longer a reality. The days of working for a company for 30-40 years and retiring with a large pension is all but disappearing. Our careers are not very predictable nor is the beginning of retirement. Because we can't rely on employers to fund our retirements, the burden is on us to plan wisely and diligently so that we are financially ready for retirement at the same time that we are physically, emotionally, and spiritually ready.

Retirement Plan Formula

A retirement plan is a formula for determining what your retirement income will be and how you will finance that income. A well-conceived retirement plan involves three important factors:

1. Establish goals. You probably have an idea of what you want your retirement to be like. Start by setting realistic goals.
   - When do you plan to retire?
   - How much will it cost to maintain an adequate standard of living?

NOTES

- Have you taken inflation into account?
- How many years of retirement income are you likely to need?

2. Count the cost. Once you have established your retirement goals, you need to determine how much you need to save each year and how much interest you need to earn. If your hoped-for lifestyle is too rich for your budget, you may have to make adjustments. Depending on your age, income, and objectives, a moderate degree of risk will likely be required to achieve your goals.

3. Maintain discipline. Knowing what the lifestyle you envision will cost, you need to establish a disciplined investment and savings program over the balance of your working years.

The worksheet at the end of the chapter entitled "Estimating Your Retirement Needs" offers you a hands-way to work through the retirement plan formula.

Other Retirement Considerations

Affects of Inflation

Inflation makes retirement a challenge because you are aiming at a moving target. It is hard to predict how much money you will need to live on in your retirement years. Even with a 4% inflation rate, something that costs $1,000 today will cost $1,480 in ten years.

NOTES

Current age/inflation rate chart

(inflation multiples needed at age 65, with rates of inflation)

Age Today	3%	4%	5%	6%
60	1.16	1.22	1.28	1.34
56	1.30	1.42	1.55	1.69
52	1.47	1.67	1.89	2.13
48	1.65	1.95	2.29	2.69
44	1.86	2.28	2.79	3.40
40	2.09	2.67	3.39	4.29

For example, if a 48 year-old person expected a four percent inflation rate, they would multiply 1.95 times what an item costs today to determine the same cost of that item when they are age 65. The solution to inflation = PLAN AHEAD!

Employer Retirement Plans

If your employer offers a retirement plan, it is important that you are fully informed about all of your options. Pay close attention to the details of the plan and make sure you are taking full advantage of the potential of the program. Qualified employer-sponsored retirement plans come in various shapes and sizes. Taking time to learn about the ones offered by your employer may reap large financial rewards.

NOTES

Unique Issues for Women

According to a *USA Today* May 29, 1996 article, women have a unique set of circumstances relative to retirement. These circumstances exist because of the following facts:

- Women, on average, live longer than men, so they typically require larger savings.
- They tend to spend fewer years working because of family responsibilities, so the amounts that they save on a regular basis needs to be larger.
- Married women can take advantage of their husband's retirement assets, but are at a disadvantage in preparing for retirement.
- Their earnings are 5/8s of what men earn and they change jobs more often.
- Women work part-time more often than men.
- Women tend to be more conservative than they should be in their savings strategies, thus limiting their investment growth potential.

Forced Retirement

Corporate restructuring has forced many individuals into early retirement. Unplanned retirement can create a financial crisis if you are unprepared. If you are forced to retire early, you may have to rethink your retirement plans because the money won't be there.

Below is a quick summary of the steps to take over time to achieve a fulfilling retirement.

1. Eliminate debt (credit cards first).
2. Create an emergency fund (approx. three months of income/expenses).

NOTES

3. Contribute to 401(k) or 403(b) retirement plans and IRAs.
4. Eliminate mortgage interest payments.
5. Create retirement assets.

It is important to save for your current needs to avoid dependence on credit and to save for your retirement. However, be aware as you save that your attitude does not turn to hoarding or that you are putting your trust in your savings rather than in God. Remember the point of financial freedom is not to serve our own needs for security, but to serve God. If we lose sight of that and accumulate savings for the sake of security or to serve our own selfish desires, then we are not actually experiencing financial freedom, just financial independence. Having enough and living with the wrong attitude is a formula for the kind of financial bondage that our friends, Fred and Alice, experienced in chapter one.

NOTES

For Application

Personal Finance Improvement Checklist

____ Determine your short-term and long-term savings objectives.

____ Add to your savings regularly (preferably through automatic payroll deductions).

____ Identify your risk tolerance from the discussion in the chapter and the quiz in this section.

____ Set up your savings plan and open or add to your savings accounts.

____ Monitor your investments, and reposition your investments to obtain higher returns when possible.

____ Identify your retirement needs and begin a plan.

____ Research moral/ethical investment options and consider investing in companies or funds that meet your moral/ethical criteria.

____ Educate yourself through reading and research on financial topics. The Internet is a helpful source of information. Use words from the list below to direct your internet searches.

- Stewardship and Money
- Financial Ministries
- Family Finance
- Managing Money
- Financial Planning
- Children and Money
- Budgeting
- Debt & Debt Consolidation
- Getting Our of Debt
- Credit Cards
- Smart Buying
- Saving
- Tithing & Giving
- Taxes
- Retirement
- IRAs
- Mutual Funds
- Mortgage Calculators
- Loan Calculators

- Godly Stewardship
- Financial Freedom
- Money Management
- Personal Finance
- Stewardship and Children
- Financial Goals
- Household Budget
- Debt reduction
- Credit
- Spending Skills
- Money Savings
- Investing
- Insurance
- Tax Planning
- Retirement Planning
- Stock Investments
- Financial Calculators
- Investment Calculators
- Financial Advisors

____ Start saving today! (even if it's $5.00)

Investment Risk Tolerance Quiz

You need to know how much investment risk you can tolerate before you can manage your money effectively and set realistic goals. It is important to consider your age, time horizon for each of your specific goals, your income and your asset base. Complete the questions below to identify your personal investing style and preferences.

For each question below, choose the answer that matches your view the closest.

A. An investment doubles in price two months after you buy it. You had originally planned to hold it for the long term. Assuming the investment hasn't changed, you:

1 ___ Sell it immediately to insure you keep the profit.
2 ___ Hold it in hopes that the value may go higher.
3 ___ Buy more of it. It may continue to rise in value.

B. You buy an investment and it falls 15 percent one month later due to a market correction, but the potential for growth still exists, you:

1 ___ Sell it immediately and get out while you can!
2 ___ Hold it, and hope it recovers.
3 ___ Buy even more of it. It's an opportunity

C. In which of these funds would you prefer to have money invested?

1 ___ A low return money market fund without much growth potential, but is steady.
2 ___ A moderate fixed rate fund with a solid Christian organization that isn't FDIC insured.
3 ___ An aggressive growth fund with great potential that has gained little over the past 6 months.

D. Which of these investments would you feel happier about?

1 ___ A certificate of deposit that saved you from losing money in a market downturn.
2 ___ An aggressive mutual fund that doubled your money.
3 ___ An aggressive stock that you picked on your own and tripled in price.

E. You're in the final round of a television game show. Here are your choices:
   1 ___ Take $1,000 in cash
   2 ___ Take a 50 percent chance at winning $4,000.
   3 ___ Take a 20 percent chance at winning $10,000.
   4 ___ Take a 5 percent chance at winning $100,000.

F. You have a chance to buy land that is rumored to be coveted by a major commercial developer. It would cost you one month's salary and your return would equal about 6 months' salary. What do you do?
   1 ___ Pass it by. It's just a rumor and too good to be true.
   2 ___ Do some research to find out if it's the "real deal."
   3 ___ Get your checkbook out and start writing.

G. A trusted friend tells you about a new oil-drilling operation in Israel's Dead Sea. He's gathering a group of investors and wants to give you a shot, too. If the projected oil levels are reached you could gain 50 times your investment. However, your friend admits the chance of success is 35 percent. What do you do?
   1 ___ Invest nothing.
   2 ___ Invest an amount equal to one month's salary.
   3 ___ Invest an amount equal to two month's salary.
   4 ___ Invest an amount equal to four month's salary.

H. What would put the biggest smile on your face?
   1 ___ Winning $100,000 in the Readers Digest Sweepstakes!
   2 ___ A $100,000 inheritance from a rich relative.
   3 ___ Earning $100,000 by risking $2,000 in the volatile stock options market.

I. You're given the option to buy stock in your company before it goes public. You might make 10-20 times your investment when it goes public, but that won't be for 3 years. What do you do?
   1 ___ Invest nothing.
   2 ___ Invest an amount equal to one month's salary.
   3 ___ Invest an amount equal to three month's salary.
   4 ___ Invest an amount equal to six month's salary.

J. Investments in which the principal is "100% safe" don't lose any money, but may lose their purchasing power. With respect to your goal(s), which of the following is most true?

1 ___ My money should be "100% safe," even if it only keeps pace with inflation.

2 ___ It's important that my investments grow faster than inflation and I am willing to accept a fair amount of risk to try to achieve this.

3 ___ My money should earn at least a 12% regardless of the risks involved.

4 ___ If I don't take major risks I can't get high returns of 15% or more.

K. Consider the following two investments, A and B. Investment A provides an average annual return of 5% with minimal risk of loss of principal. Investment B provides an average annual return of 10%, but carries a potential loss of principal of 20% or more in any one year. If you could choose between Investment A and Investment B to meet your goal(s), how would you invest your money:

1 ___ 80% in Investment A and 20% in Investment B.

2 ___ 50% in Investment A and 50% in Investment B.

3 ___ 20% in Investment A and 80% in Investment B.

4 ___ 0% in Investment A and 100% in Investment B.

L. How would your spouse or best friend describe you as a risk-taker?

1 ___ Risk averse.

2 ___ Cautious.

3 ___ Willing to take risks after doing some research.

4 ___ Has a risk-taking reputation and proud of it.

Results

Now, total up your score by adding up the number of responses to each number in the twelve questions above, multiply them by number listed below, then add the subtotals to get your score:

# of Ones	___	x 1 =	___
# of Twos	___	x 2 =	___
# of Threes	___	x 3 =	___
# of Fours	___	x 4 =	___
Total Score			___

Score 12-16   Conservative - In this risk category, preservation of capital is your single most important concern. Adjusted for inflation, investment returns may be very low or, in some years, negative, in exchange for very high liquidity and minimal risk of principal loss.

Score 17-24   Moderate - Investors in this risk category accept possible principal loss as a natural function of investment risk in the pursuit of higher average annual total returns. The degree of risk is normally reduced through diversification and adjusting the mix/choice of funds based upon market expectations.

Score 25-32   Moderate to Aggressive - Investors in this category are more willing to take risk, both in types of investments held and market sectors, accepting possible loss of principal. More active portfolio adjustment is a typical feature of this type of investor behavior.

Score 33-42   Aggressive - Investors in this risk category typically are more willing to accept losses in pursuit of overall portfolio results that historically produce higher average annual total returns. This type of investor may speculate more, make frequent portfolio changes, and experience a wide variance in returns from one year to the next in the pursuit of longer-term goals.

Estimate Your Retirement Needs

This worksheet is designed to help you think through the various aspects of retirement planning and to estimate your financial requirements at retirement. This will help you set some goals today so you can achieve your needs in the future.

1. Determine the retirement income you desire (between 70-80 % of current income).

2. Determine the age you want your retirement to begin.

3. Find out what your Social Security benefit will be at the age of your retirement.

4. Find out your employer's retirement plan benefits at retirement age (if applicable).

5. Calculate potential income from other sources (sale of property or business, personal investments, savings, and charitable trusts/annuities.) These will represent a major source of retirement income.

6. Add benefits from 3, 4, and 5 to determine the total value of your assets at retirement:

   Social Security   _____

   Employer Retirement plan(s)   +_____

   Other income potential   + _____

   Personal Investments/Savings   + _____

   Total Potential Assets   =   _____

7. Estimate how much additional money you will need to save to achieve your goals by determining the following:
   - The number of years left to save for retirement.
   - The amount of additional money you can contribute to your retirement fund.
   - The estimated rate of compounded interest.
   - The number of years you expect to draw retirement income.

8.   Calculate your inflation factor from the chart in this chapter.

Reflections on Saving

1. **Read Proverbs 11:28 and Mark 10:17-22** and evaluate your attitude toward saving. Are you putting your trust in your savings rather than in God? If so, pray to Him now and ask His forgiveness and to redirect your focus to Him alone as your source of security.

2. **Read the parable in Luke 12:13-21** and examine your attitude about retirement. Do you see yourself spending all of your time indulging in your self-interests, or do you see yourself serving God and others in a new and different capacity? How has this scripture and the information in the chapter impacted your view of your own retirement?

   _____

   _____

   _____

   _____

3. God has provided for us through work, saving, and prayer (chapter two). What are the consequences of _not_ putting your money to work through saving and investing according to the parable in **Matthew 25:14-30**?

   _____

   _____

   _____

4. Additional Scriptures for review and reflection:
   Job 31:24-28, Psalm 33:20-22, Psalm 49:12-13

   Prayer: _Lord, thank you for your provision for me through saving. I confess that I have not saved as I should because I am living for the desires of today with no thought for the future. I want to change my focus to be a better steward of the funds that you provide me today so that I will able to meet life's expected and unexpected financial demands without incurring more debt and so that I can be free in my retirement to serve you with more of my time._

CHAPTER 7

Giving -
The Foundation for Financial Freedom

"A tithe of everything from the land...
Lev. 27:30

We have discussed a lot of details to manage our personal financial situations through the practical applications of budgeting, debt management, and the principles of spending and saving. If you have worked through some of the worksheets and quizzes, you are hopefully feeling pretty encouraged that getting out of debt and on the road toward financial freedom is, indeed, possible — even if you are currently buried in debt. Now that there is "light at the end of the tunnel," let's set our focus on the primary purpose for financial freedom, which is freedom to serve God. As the title of this chapter suggests, the foundation for financial freedom truly is giving. We are talking about the obedient practice of paying the tithe faithfully, as well as giving of our time, possessions, and sacrificial gifts.

"Give, and it will be given to you. A good measure, pressed down, shaken together and running over, will be poured into your lap. For with the measure you use, it will be measured to you."

Luke 6:38

Givers and Takers

Someone has said there are two kinds of people in the world — givers and takers. "Takers" are those people who think of themselves first. They look for others to give to them, and they have a hard time sharing what they have with others. Often they feel like they are not getting their fair share. Some will even

NOTES

cheat to get or keep more. Takers are seldom content and always want more, even coveting what others have. If they do give, it is usually the minimum and often grudgingly or to impress others.

"Givers" are those people who think of others first. They look for opportunities to share their time and resources because they just want to give. They tend to be involved in their church and community. They feel grateful for what they have. In fact, the more they get, the more they give. While striving to be all they can be and looking to maximize their wealth, they are contented with where they are at the moment. Their reason for making more wealth is to give more away. Givers are those that have discovered that the act of giving brings greater joy than does receiving.

Take the "Do I Have A Giving Mentality?" quiz at the end of the chapter to discover if you lean more toward being a giver or a taker. Whichever category you fall into, you will benefit from the biblical and practical principles that are outlined in the rest of this chapter.

Stewardship vs. Ownership

I love the story my pastor tells about his first pickup truck. He was 16 years old and had been saving for five years for the day when he could own and drive his own truck. Admonition from his father about the cost of driving a truck, the cost of up-keep, and the risk involved with ownership fell on deaf ears. The day came when he purchased the truck. My, how his perspective changed! He said that rather than feeling joy at owning the truck, he remembers the overwhelming feeling of burden and the sense of responsibility he felt in "being the one in charge" rather than the feeling of freedom and personal power he had anticipated. He remembers saying to his father, "It was so much easier when you

NOTES

owned the truck, and all I did was borrow it."

Understanding the difference between stewardship and ownership is key here. A steward is the person placed in charge of someone else's affairs. As Christians, we have control of our lives, our money and all of our belongings, but God is the owner. As owner, God takes full responsibility (as the Father, He owns the truck). He gives us direction and guidelines to follow (His Word) and then leaves the management to us.

Does God Really Need My Money?

Though most of us are keenly aware that God doesn't need our money, sometimes it is important to remind ourselves of that fact. God does ask us to give our money, our time, or our personal gifts/talents in order to bring blessing in the church. We are His people. He wants to be able to give us direction and to have us willingly and cheerfully obey Him in the area of giving, but God can accomplish His mission with or without us.

> *"Remember this: Whoever sows sparingly will also reap sparingly, and whoever sows generously will also reap generously... God love's a cheerful giver."*
>
> 2 Corinthians 9:6-7

2 Corinthians 9:6 promises that if we sow even a tiny amount of faith, we will reap enormous spiritual results. It is by exercising our faith in giving that we are able to sow generously and also reap generously.

Paul says that if you sow generously, *"You will be made rich in every way so that you can be generous on every occasion..."* (2 Cor. 9:11) Do not confuse this with the "health-and-wealth, prosperity gospel" because God's Word defines rich as "able to be generous." And that is not necessarily translated into

NOTES

an abundance of cash in His economy. However, it is easy to understand why God supplies more than our basic needs when viewed from the perspective of giving.

God's Plan for Our Giving

The Old Testament gives us the first look at God's plan for giving in Leviticus 27:30, *"A tithe of everything from the land."* God wanted a portion given automatically back to Him as a sign of trust, obedience and faith in His care and provision. Tithing was fundamental in the Jewish life and culture. In New Testament times when Jesus said to His followers, *"I have come to complete the Law not abolish it,"* the listener clearly understood the tithe was to continue as part of the believer's life practice. Jesus knew the people He was talking with understood the tithe, so it wasn't even necessary for Him to revisit this teaching but rather to expand on it. In Matthew 23:23, Jesus remarked about the Pharisees' strict adherence to the laws of the tithe, even with the most insignificant of their possessions, yet they neglected larger issues of true justice and mercy. Jesus did not rebuke them for their devoted attitude toward the tithe. If He had wished to retract the necessity of tithing, this would have been a great place for Him to say, "Your tithe is useless."

Jesus was sent as God's "gift" to mankind providing atonement for our sins. And today, when Jesus Christ becomes our personal savior, we are expected to follow the same course–begin with a tithe and then move on to special-need giving as God leads.

When we choose to give 10% of our gross income back to God, we demonstrate our reliance on Him as the source of all of our blessings. It is common today for Christians to debate whether we're still required to tithe, but that's

NOTES

the wrong argument. The question we ought to be asking is, "Does the promise of Malachi 3:10-12 still apply today?" If we *"bring the whole tithe into the storehouse,"* will God still *"throw open [for us] the floodgates of heaven, and pour out so much blessing that [we] will not have room enough for it."*

Before you answer, consider God's declaration in Malachi 3:6, " I, the Lord, do not change," and Hebrews 13:8, *"Jesus Christ is the same yesterday and today, yes and forever."* When considering this question, we need to also make sure that we don't reduce His blessings to only material stuff.

Guidelines for Tithing and Giving

As Christians, we are admonished to give above and beyond our tithe. The materialistic bent of our contemporary society makes it difficult to establish giving as a top priority. But hopefully through the principles that you have learned through previous chapters of this book, you will recognize that giving can become a top priority and that it is a mark of financial freedom. An excellent illustration that teaches the principle of tithing is found in "Money Clues for the Clueless." [1]

A Picture of Tithing Written in Chocolate

If you want to get a good picture of God's view of tithing, think about the well-worn illustration of the box of candy. Imagine that you go to visit a child and take her a box of candy. In one scenario the child thanks you for the gift and then opens the box and says, "Would you like the first piece?" That is a picture of biblical giving. In another scenario, the child grabs the box, hides out

---

[1] Money Clues for the Clueless, Compilation, Promise Press, 2000, page 44

NOTES

in her room for a while and then finally comes out to where you are sitting. With chocolate smeared all over her face, she offers you a piece of the candy that she didn't want. That is not a picture of godly giving. The first picture recognizes the source of the gift. When we tithe that is exactly what we are doing: recognizing God as the Source of the good things in our lives.

Giving is a by-product of our faith and an outward sign of our priorities and our hearts. If we put God first in our lives, He promises to meet our needs (Matt. 6:33). Here are some specific principles and promises found in scripture relative to giving and tithing.

GIVE FIRST FRUITS

1. *"Honor the Lord with your wealth, with the firstfruits of all your crops."* (Prov. 3:9) This principle doesn't just apply to crops, but also to income. The "God First" principle means that we give to God the first part of our incomes. By doing so, we are reminded of God's ownership. I have made it a practice to write the tithe check as the first action after depositing my paycheck.

2. Making our giving a priority confirms the trust we place in God. However, following this principle doesn't automatically assure us of financial prosperity. We are called to fit into God's plans, rather than for God to fit into ours.

3. We all face situations where we could use our money for purposes other than the Lord's. When money gets tight, our obedience to God is tested.

NOTES

GIVE PROPORTIONATELY

1. This means to give in proportion to the income we receive, not giving a specific dollar amount. *"Each one of you should set aside a sum of money in keeping with his income"* (1 Cor.16: 2).

2. Deuteronomy 16:17 says, *"Each of you must bring a gift in proportion to the way the Lord your God has blessed you."* Proportionate giving challenges both the rich and the poor.

3. The growth of your portfolio or your net worth should be included in your calculation of your tithe according to Deuteronomy 14:22, which says, *"You shall truly tithe all the increase of your grain that the field produces year by year."* (NKJV)

GIVE SACRIFICIALLY

1. *"Out of their most severe trial, their overflowing joy and their extreme poverty welled up in rich generosity. For I testify that they gave as much as they were able, and even beyond their ability."* (2 Cor. 8:2-3)

Giving sacrificially usually includes one of the following:
- A rearrangement of priorities
- A change in lifestyle
- Giving up something of value

2. When we give sacrificially, we give our best. As our faith matures we offer God more and more choice portions of our treasures.

NOTES

3. The Widow at Zarephath in 1 Kings 17:7-24 demonstrated sacrificial giving. She went to her cupboards, which were already lean, and found food for someone in need. Out of obedience and love for God, the widow was willing to give up the last of her bread. Because of her generosity, she and her son survived the famine.

4. Giving things that we don't want or need is not sacrificial giving. Sacrificial giving is sharing what we would rather keep.

GIVE REGULARLY

1. Many people give a tithe each and every Sunday out of habit, which is biblical. *"On the first day of every week, each one of you should set aside a sum of money in keeping with his income, saving it up, so that when I come no collections will have to be made."* (1 Cor. 16:2)

2. Our giving becomes regular when we are committed to giving our first fruits. If we are inclined to give the leftovers each month, we often will have nothing left to give, and our giving becomes irregular. Failure to give is a spiritual problem, not a financial one.

GIVE CHEERFULLY

1. *"It is more blessed to give than to receive."* (Acts 20:35)

2. *"Each man should give what he has decided in his heart, not reluctantly or under compulsion, for God loves a cheerful giver."* (2 Cor. 9:7)

NOTES

3. The tithe is not an offering. The Bible speaks of it being "brought" and "presented" or "paid" rather than given. Voluntary or freewill offerings are contributions in addition to the tithe. They constitute, perhaps, what true giving is all about because they are evidence of a heart full of love, joy, and worship for God. Offerings come from a spirit of cheerful giving.

GIVE QUIETLY

1. We are proud by nature. However, God teaches us to give without a public display because the glory should go to God, not to ourselves. (Matt. 6:3-4)

2. *"Be careful not to do your acts of righteousness before men, to be seen by them. If you do, you will have no reward from your Father in heaven."* (Matt. 6:1)

In the Old Testament the tithe was brought to the storehouse to do the Lord's work. Tithe to your home congregation to underwrite the ministry of the local church, to support your pastor, and to provide for the needs of the less fortunate in your community [Deut.14: 27-29]. Beyond your tithe, seek counsel from your pastor and others who would have specific knowledge about other ministries, missionaries, and para-church organizations that you want to support with your offerings. Be thoughtful and careful. Take time to pray and ask God to guide you, heeding the counsel in Proverbs 28:27, which says, *"He who gives to the poor will lack nothing, but he who closes his eyes to them receives many curses."*

Debbie's story illustrates that when we practice biblical giving, we open the door for God to provide for us and for others through us.

NOTES

As a young youth pastor struggling to make ends meet, Debbie wanted to be open to whatever the Lord asked of her. Early in her Christian life Debbie committed to tithing and, in response to her commitment, faithfully gave one-tenth of her income monthly to her church. One month she was down to the last twelve dollars in her checking account, and payday was a week away. Debbie felt the Lord prompting her to use her twelve dollars to buy groceries for a needy family in her church and to trust the Lord to provide for her own needs. She bought the groceries, the family was blessed by this special provision from God, and the Lord helped Debbie make it to payday without any problems.

Debbie's experience began with obedience to God by paying her tithe. She believed that God could and would provide for her. When she saw how God provided for her and through her, it opened the door to one of the most powerful aspects of giving. She experienced God's miraculous provision, as well as the freedom and joy that comes from being generous and open to His leading. More fundamentally, she entered into her relationship with God as a steward rather than as an owner.

When we tithe, it demonstrates our understanding of Jesus' words, *"It is better to give than to receive."* (Acts 20:35) God asks His children to tithe in obedience to His Word, thus allowing His resources to work their way back to us in unexpected and bountiful ways.

Tithing teaches us to put God first in our lives so that we learn to revere Him always, as Deuteronomy 14:23 instructs. Giving God our first fruits is a reminder that we owe all that we have to God. After all, God owns it all and only asks us to give Him a tenth of it. He allows us to keep the remainder as a testament to our stewardship.

Tithing is a great opportunity to test God's promise to provide. As human

---

NOTES

beings, we tend to focus on material blessing and enter into a race to "keep up" with our neighbors. God's Word encourages us with, *"Be content with what you have, because God said, Never will I leave you, never will I forsake you."* (Heb. 13:5) We don't need to strive to keep up with others, but rather to have lives committed to the Lordship of Christ.

Teaching Children About Giving

Passing the joys of being a faithful steward and a life of financial freedom to our children is a key responsibility for parents and one of the great gifts that we can give to our kids. If giving is the foundation for financial freedom, then it is essential to teach children to develop this value. The tithe portion of the child's bank is a starting place for teaching this biblical principle, but beyond the tithe, there will be a number of opportunities throughout the child's life to experience the gift of giving in a variety of ways. When we model a spirit of giving to our children (through service to the church, giving to missions and other special needs, volunteering in civic or charitable organizations, etc.), we underscore for them that the things we have from God are to be used for His purpose and glory. It is one thing to write a check, but how do our children involve themselves in that activity or even relate to it? It is much more tangible for them to experience working alongside you in a volunteer capacity, or to go through their own toy box to find items that they would like to give to a cause.

Giving is an action and an attitude that our children can observe and emulate in their formative years. Since it involves more than just money, anyone can demonstrate a lifestyle of giving through their time, talents and possessions as well. Just as my mother demonstrated to me so many years ago when I felt that we didn't have enough to give, but she gave anyway, we also can demonstrate that to our children today.

NOTES

Giving as God Leads

A full experience in giving involves both tithes and offerings. We should give our full tithe to our home church. It is the storehouse, and God's primary instrument in reaching the lost and equipping you for evangelism. Beyond that ten percent, we should give as the Lord leads to special needs, missionaries, building projects, etc. Over the years, I have found it exciting and fulfilling to be available to the Holy Spirit as He leads our family to respond to special needs. A few years ago the Holy Spirit challenged Connie and me to take a look at our possessions and ask God if we should give anything to support ministry or for the benefit of someone in need. We felt led to donate our van, and the decision became a family affair. We took the van to the church, explained how God was leading, asked that our gift be anonymous, then waited to see what God would do. The next Sunday night our pastor surprised a young missionary and his family with a van for their ministry. I can still see the looks of awe and joy on the faces of our children as they heard the announcement and realized God had used our family to supply a very special need. God may not "need" our money or possessions to accomplish His purpose, but our faith is certainly strengthened when we obey His lead and experience the miraculous way only God can use us to help someone else.

This service that you perform is not only supplying the needs of God's people, but is also overflowing in many expressions of thanks to God.
II Cor. 9:12

On another occasion I remember sitting in a church service when an appeal was made for the salary needs of a missionary pastor. I didn't know him personally, so I sat there half listening. Before long I realized the Lord was nudging me to meet the need. I didn't hear an audible voice, but the message was

NOTES

clear in my mind, "I want to use you to provide this need." The choice was mine, to give or not to give. I did choose to give my money, and later my time, to help the pastor with a financial plan for the church. Sometimes when we are His, and allow Him to use us to provide for others, it is hard to tell who gets the greatest blessing, the one giving or the one receiving. *"Remember this: Whoever sows sparingly will also reap sparingly, and whosoever sows generously will also reap generously. Each man should give what he has decided in his heart to give, not reluctantly or under compulsion, for God loves a cheerful giver."* (II Cor. 9:6, 7)

Giving to the Less Fortunate

The most powerful admonition regarding giving to others in need is found in 1 John 3:17, *"If anyone has material possessions and sees his brother in need, but has no pity on him, how can the love of God be in him?"* When you help the poor you are demonstrating God's love. Nothing feels better than putting skin on Jesus for someone.

For me the process of giving to those who are less fortunate goes something like this:

- I am committed to being a faithful and responsive steward.
- God reminds me that He is my provider and that His provisions extend beyond my needs.
- I ask God to help me love others in a practical way by recognizing the needs of others.
- I take notice of people who are in need and have genuine compassion and empathy for them.
- God prompts me to give out of the excess He has provided.
- I give and experience true joy and fulfillment as an obedient steward.

NOTES

- I allow my life to be an example to inspire others to be faithful stewards and give as God directs. Jesus Himself told us, *"Freely you have received, freely give."* (Matt. 10:8)

Tithing on the Increase Through Planned Giving

Earlier in this chapter in the discussion about giving proportionately, I referenced Deuteronomy 14:22, which talks about "tithing on the increase." Putting this counsel into practice can be difficult if we don't understand what the "increase" is or how we can tithe on it. Our "income" is what we receive in exchange for our labor, and we are taught to pay our tithe on those funds immediately and regularly. Our "increase" is the growth in value on our investments and assets. Most Americans don't begin to liquidate their real estate, IRA, 401(k), and other investments until they reach retirement. That means that they never really have access to even a portion of the increase until then — and have typically planned to use those funds to live on for the remainder of their lives. Therefore, tithing on one's increase is overlooked and many times it never happens. Consider your personal residence as another example. You may buy and sell a number of times, and each time reinvest the entire amount (which includes the appreciation you gained on the asset). With both of these scenarios you have little chance to tithe on the increase.

Your first key opportunity to tithe on the increase of your assets is probably through your estate plan. That is why many people decide to give a percentage of their estate assets to their local church and other ministries at death through their will or living trust. Others create charitable trusts using estate assets such as real estate, stocks, mutual funds, IRAs, pension plans, etc. By doing so, they are assured of a stable lifetime income and leave the asset balance

NOTES

upon death to the ministries of their choosing. Charitable trusts can also be used to gift assets that are no longer needed to one or more ministries for a period of time, and then have them transferred to family members and others. Either way, the individual receives a charitable tax deduction and honors God with their tithe. This concept in general is called "planned giving" and is a very practical way to fulfill the scripture's call to tithe on the increase as well as to leave a lasting ministry legacy.

My intent in this section is to bring this subject to your attention and to inform you of a variety of possibilities for tithing on the increase. However, there are so many different ways to arrange your estate to accomplish the objectives of caring for your family and giving to the Lord that the best advice is to seek counsel in this area of stewardship. Attorneys and CPAs are equipped to assist you in arranging these affairs, but they may not necessarily have your stewardship intent in mind when they are counseling you.

What feelings are associated with giving? I have heard people say, "I felt so much joy when I was using my voice for the Lord," or "I felt the quietness of God's voice in my heart and I knew I should give to the church building project." Sometimes the joy of the Lord shows on the faces of His children, and their faithfulness for His work becomes contagious. I urge you to open your heart and spirit to what God may be saying to you about your personal and family giving. God wants you to put Him to the test in this area of life. When you do, you will discover that financial freedom really is more than being debt free.

NOTES

For Application
Personal Finance Improvement Checklist

____ If you haven't started tithing, begin now, and thank God for the opportunity to give.

____ If you have been tithing on your net income, ask God to give you the courage and discipline to begin tithing on your gross.

____ List your needs, pray about them with your family, and ask God to meet your needs.

____ Memorize scriptures to increase your faith and help you trust Him with your finances.

____ Consider a charitable gift ("planned gift") in your estate plan as a way to tithe on the increase of your assets and investments.

Do I Have A "Giving" Mentality Quiz: (Circle One)

1. I get more joy out of giving gifts to others than I do receiving gifts myself.	True False
2. I often find myself fixing a meal or making some other gesture for others in need.	True False
3. I have participated in some activity to help the needy in my community this past year.	True False
4. I have been known to take in stray animals and give them food and shelter.	True False
5. I have faithfully given a tithe each month to God this past year.	True False
6. I tithe on my gross income rather than my net income.	True False
7. In addition to my tithe, I have given to at least one charity or religious organization outside my church this past year. (Billy Graham, March of Dimes, American Cancer Society, United Way, etc.)	True False
8. When I give money, time, or possessions, I do not think about what I "may" or "should" receive in return. I do not "keep score."	True False
10. I belong to at least one civic organization in my community. (Rotary or other service club, Habitat for Humanity, Boys and Girls Club, Big Brother/Sister, Hospice, etc.)	True False
11. I am actively involved in at least one volunteer ministry in my local church that requires faithful and consistent giving of my time.	True False

Results: The more "true" answers you have, the more you tend to possess a true "giver" mentality. The more "false" answers you have, the more you tend to possess a "taker" mentality.

Reflections on Giving

1. Take a moment to reflect on your habits of giving. Be honest. Do you find in yourself the basic tendency to be a "giver" or "taker?" If you discover that you are more of a taker, confess this to God and ask Him to help you change.

2. **Read II Corinthians 9:6-8.** What has your attitude about tithing and giving been in the past? Have you viewed it as an obligation, an offensive request by the pastor, or as an opportunity to express your faith in God? Have your thoughts changed since reading this chapter? If so, write those changes below. _____

   _____

   _____

3. If you do not currently tithe, read **Leviticus 27:30 and Malachi 3:7-12** and commit to start tithing right away. Ask God to help you overcome the fear of not having enough and to help you to have the courage to give regularly.

4. If your tithing patterns are sporadic, are you truly putting God first as **Proverbs 3:9** says? Consider the various things that you can do to make tithing a priority in your life. Review the chapter for suggestions and write your action plan here.

   _____

   _____

   _____

5. Go back and review the "Guidelines for Giving" section of the chapter about giving regularly, proportionately, sacrificially, etc. Are there any areas in your current attitudes and practices that need correction? List those areas below and talk with God about your desire to change.

    _____

    _____

    _____

6. Do you ever take the opportunity to give beyond your tithe? Is this something that you would like to do but don't feel able because of tight finances? Ask God to help you in your financial journey so that you can release finances for His work beyond your tithe. This is truly where financial freedom is best expressed in our hearts and lives. **Read Matthew 6:1-4, Proverbs 3:27-28, and Luke 6:38** for guidelines for giving.

7. Additional Scriptures for review and reflection:
    Psalm 37:25-26, Proverbs 11:229 and 24-26, Luke 21:1-4,
    I Timothy 6:17-19

Prayer: *Lord, thank you for giving me the opportunity to express my faith in you through the tithe and to demonstrate your love for others through the gift of giving. I want to be a faithful giver, but I need your help to overcome my fears of not having enough. I commit today to make my tithe the first check that I write after my next payday and each payday after that, and I will trust You to provide for the difference. Amen.*

CHAPTER 8

Managing Your Estate

Wise estate planning removes the worry of leaving your family in financial hardship and also keeps you focused on your stewardship goals.

Don't Stop Now!

So many people hear the term, "Estate Planning," and they immediately yawn and want to just go to sleep because the topic seems "so boring." Or they see the words "Estate Planning" and their eyes glaze over and they skim or skip the section. In fact, you are probably tempted to do that now, especially since you are at the last chapter of the book. You've done the hard work of trying to make a plan toward financial freedom. So hey, you've gotten what you came for, right?

Let me encourage you to keep reading for a few pages longer. It would be so unfortunate for you to work hard to live in financial freedom only to lose it at your death or unfortunate disability simply for lack of planning. These next few pages are designed to give you an overview of the issues of managing and transferring your God-given estate. It is not a college course, by any means, it is just designed to give you enough information to begin the process.

Estate Planning is a Process, not an Event

Mr. and Mrs. Thompson attended an estate-planning seminar that Dave conducted at their church and later requested a personal consultation with him. In that meeting, they discovered that their wills were outdated and they had an invalid revocable living trust. The Thompsons did not realize that estate plan-

NOTES

ning is an ongoing activity throughout one's lifetime and not just a single event.

They also did not know that they could structure their assets to reduce or avoid some taxes as well as to deter potential family conflict. Dave outlined a number of tools available to create additional retirement income, transfer assets to family and ministries they support, and offered a variety of other suggestions for issues that they were facing.

In one brief meeting with a knowledgeable professional, Mr. and Mrs. Thompson gained a new understanding of the estate planning process, established clear stewardship objectives, and resolved most of the problems that existed in their current estate plan.

The majority of Americans are like the Thompsons with a limited understanding of the purpose and the process of estate planning. So many people base their attitudes and actions upon tradition (how it's always been done) rather than on learning and discerning what God's plan is for their estate as a part of their total life of stewardship. If you relate to the Thompsons' story, then you can benefit from reading this chapter.

Estate Planning Defined

Your estate consists of all of the assets and liabilities you have during your life and at the time of your death. Estate planning begins with the first money and/or possessions you acquire. Just as with building a home, you first begin saving, gathering information, selecting a plan, and then continuing until the project is complete. Therefore, estate planning is the creation, conservation, and utilization of estate resources to secure the maximum benefit now, during disability and at retirement. It is the best way to pass one's assets to family members, ministry organizations, and others during life and at death, with min-

---

NOTES

imum shrinkage caused by taxes and inflation.

At one time, people regarded estate planning as a concern only for the wealthy, but today anyone who owns anything should develop a plan. Wise use of available estate planning techniques and tools can be of considerable benefit to you. Planning will take away the worry of leaving your family in financial hardship and also keep you focused on your stewardship goals.

Estate Planning in the Christian Context

For the Christian, estate planning is typically the most important act of stewardship he or she will ever undertake. This characterization recognizes that God is the owner of all (including our estates) and places us in positions as stewards to responsibly manage the estate in our care. During every step of the estate planning process it is important for stewards to keep in mind these biblical principles:

- God is the owner of all. (Psalm 50:12)
- The first priority of all estate asset transfers is to provide for individuals and ministries who are financially dependent on us, and the primary motivation for giving must be love. (John 3:16)
- People are more important than money and things, so putting inter-personal relationships at risk is destructive and thoughtless. (I Tim. 5:8)
- It is required of a servant to place a higher priority on spiritual issues over financial ones. (Matt. 24:45-51) Every financial decision has spiritual implications and reflects our spiritual priorities.
- A steward is a caretaker, trustee, or custodian of someone else's property. (Matt. 25:14-30).

NOTES

As stewards it is important that we use our estate assets, both large and small, to their fullest potential during our lifetimes for our personal, family, business and ministry interests. Prior to death, we must arrange for the efficient and effective transfer to our assets to individuals and/or ministries who will continue to use them to reflect our Christian beliefs and lifestyles after we are gone.

Planning for Yourself and Your Family

When we talk about managing and transferring our estate, we think primarily of prearranging our affairs for the benefit of family and other individual and ministry-related beneficiaries after our death.

Your highest priority in estate planning should be to care and provide for the people dearest to you. In I Timothy 5:8 Paul says, *"If anyone does not provide for his relatives, and especially for his immediate family, he has denied the faith and is worse than an unbeliever."*

Faithful and thoughtful management of your finances and property is important, but it is never wise to allow issues related to those decisions to create conflict between you and your loved ones or amongst themselves. Money and possessions, no matter how great, are not more important than people. But unfortunately, in the United States estate assets are often distributed in a manner that causes conflict between family and friends, and in many of those situations the conflict is never fully resolved.

We have all heard stories about individuals and couples who are committed to faithful stewardship, work very hard their entire lifetime, and then leave all their wealth to their children. When they die, their children inherit everything their parents had, and it either spoils them, ruins their lives, or they squander all they are given. Why does this happen?

NOTES

The scripture tells us in Proverbs 22:6 to *"train a child in the way he should go, and when he is old he will not turn from it."* We all recognize that we have the responsibility to train our kids in the ways of the Lord, but what about leaving resources to help them fulfill their God-given calling in the world? Proverbs 13:22 says, *"A good man leaves an inheritance for his children's children, but a sinner's wealth is stored up for the righteous."* As Christians we are responsible to plan for our own needs now and in the future, and perhaps leave something for our children as well.

One of the greatest joys I have as a father is to know my children have the Lord Jesus Christ as their Savior, they serve Him as Lord, and from an early age they practice His principles of stewardship. Children learn by example by being shown how to do things and then helped with follow through. When we have properly trained our children, it is a privilege to plan and save knowing they will have the fruits of our labors when our life on earth ends.

Some Concepts to Consider

There are several common errors made by parents and grandparents today relative to planning their estates. First of all, tradition has taught people to believe that they are obligated to leave their entire estate to their children and grandchildren. Secondly, people have the mistaken belief that the eldest child should be the executor (personal representative) of the estate. Thirdly, parents and grandparents have the false impression that their written will is a sufficient estate plan. And finally, people just simply procrastinate or don't believe that they have enough to justify an estate plan.

Let's address these errors one by one. It is my hope to arm you with some foundational principles that will assist you in the decision-making processes of

NOTES

planning your estate. You see, I believe that estate planning is first spiritual and then mechanical. Meaning, first there must be a good understanding of biblical stewardship principles, priorities, and responsibilities, and then all of the detailed decisions will be made from that spiritual perspective. These are concepts you would not likely hear from your financial advisor or attorney.

Error 1: I have an obligation to leave my entire estate to my offspring.

It is true that scripture obligates us to provide for our dependent spouse and children. However, scripture does not say to do so excessively and not necessarily if our grown children are not living in a manner that will continue your service to the Lord's purposes after your death. This concept is expressed in the combination of points that were just made about stewardship — arranging our estate assets to provide for our loved ones and ministries we believe in and to transfer them in ways that reflect our Christian beliefs.

An illustration of this concept is clear in the case of my friend, "Jack." Jack is a wealthy Christian man who has determined to leave a portion of his estate to his only son as a way of provision for his son's future. However, his son is not living for the Lord, and so Jack will not leave everything to the son. As a steward of God's provision, and out of a sense of a duty in his service to God, Jack feels a higher obligation to ensure that God's provision for him on earth is used in Christ's service after Jack's death. So, after the portion that is left to the son, Jack plans to bless a ministry that espouses his values with the majority of his estate.

There are no hard and fast rules for transferring your estate assets. However, by following "traditional" estate planning guidelines where you leave all or a majority of estate assets to family regardless of your relationship with

---

NOTES

them or their understanding of bibilical stewardship beliefs and practices, or out of guilt, you may be missing God's plan of stewardship for distributing your estate.

Error 2: My eldest child should be the executor of my estate. That's just how it's done.

Parents may have good intentions by naming a child as executor (also referred to as a personal representative), but it may be better to name a neutral party that is unemotionally involved and won't be a beneficiary of estate assets. The responsibility of executor can be more of a burden than a benefit to the siblings — especially when there are differing opinions and differing levels of relationship among them. Our friend, "Sharon," is a co-executor of her parents' estate (father and step-mother). She says that she wishes her folks would have named a neutral party to manage the estate. It has been over six years since their simultaneous death in an accident, and she is still struggling with strained sibling relationships (both her own siblings and step-siblings) surrounding financial decisions that need to be made regarding the property that was left in the estate. If you have more than one child and wish to name one as your executor, the wisest way would be to name two children as co-executors so they are required to work as a team and possibly keep each other accountable. Remember, your goal is to make arrangements to avoid interpersonal conflicts at all costs. You also want to avoid placing the burden of responsibility upon the shoulders of only one child.

Error 3: I have a written will, and that is sufficient to let my loved ones know my desires.

A Last Will and Testament is a first step in prearranging an estate, but it

NOTES

is insufficient in itself to handle all of the issues surrounding the transfer and ownership of assets, handling estate taxes, etc. There is more detail about the mechanics of a will later in this chapter.

Error 4: Procrastination

This is the number one reason people give for not doing an estate plan. When it comes to this critical phase of life planning people procrastinate because it seems too difficult, cumbersome or expensive. Here are a variety of reasons people postpone or avoid making a will or estate plan. Do you recognize your own reasons in this list?

I'm Superstitious. Some people avoid discussing anything associated with death for fear that it will occur sooner.

I feel apathetic. "I'll be gone, so who cares?" God and your family care. Providing for your family spiritually, materially, and emotionally is a genuine sign of your love for them.

I'm young and have plenty of time. You may think that you have plenty of time, but your time and life are in God's hands. And accidents do happen to both the young and old.

Everything I own is in joint ownership. If you own everything in joint tenancy with your spouse, everything outside of probate will automatically go to your surviving spouse at your death. This is an effective estate asset transfer technique, but is not a cure all. It doesn't address estate planning at the

---

NOTES

death of the surviving spouse, or a disaster that results in a simultaneous death.

Estate planning is only for the wealthy, or "I can't afford a will." Most people can't afford not to write a will. The added time and expense to settle an estate without a will is much greater. A will can be created for around $125, and the peace of mind that you have taken care of an important stewardship responsibility is well worth it. Or, consider it from this perspective: For a cost of less than 1% of your assets you can effectively protect and transfer them.

If you identify yourself in any of these excuses, then make the time to do it! You don't have to do all your estate planning at once — take it one step at a time starting with the writing or revision of your will. Procrastination can be hazardous to your God-entrusted wealth!

Purposes of Estate Planning

Upon death your accumulated assets will go to your family, the government, or ministry. If you properly plan, you can determine what percentage of your assets end up in the hands of these entities. If you don't properly plan, the IRS will take as much as they possibly can from your estate and the government will decide how it spends your hard-earned money. A thoughtful and well-designed estate plan can effectively provide for your family into the future, benefit a church, ministry, or cause that you care about, and reduce your tax liabilities. In addition, estate plans are valuable for a number of other reasons (both spiritual and economical) outlined in the following list.

NOTES

- Convey your love for the Lord, your family and your friends.
- Preserve and utilize assets for short- and long-term personal needs.
- Convert non-liquid assets into liquid assets so they are easily distributed.
- Ensure that your assets are distributed they way you want them to be.
- Distribute assets without creating interpersonal family conflicts.
- Minimize the time and hassle of transferring estate assets.
- Provide for the management of one's estate in case of mental or physical disability.
- Keep taxes (estate, income, capital gains, etc), probate and other administration costs to a minimum.
- Make funds available or accessible to pay death expenses, taxes and other bills.
- Provide for the continuation of the Lord's work through your local church and other ministries.
- Leave a lasting Godly legacy.

The Mechanics of Estate Planning

Remember when we said that estate planning is first spiritual and then mechanical? With the foundation established for why intentional Christian stewards plan, and having identified our reasons for not already having a plan in place, we are ready to jump into an overview of the nuts and bolts of putting an estate plan together.

Estate planning is an important tool, but it is a process that takes time. It involves money, possessions, spouses, children, grandchildren, close friends, favorite family members, your local church and other ministries or organizations. It also involves taxes, insurance policies, lawyers, banks, accountants, and financial planners.

NOTES

At a minimum, an estate plan should attend to the expenses that are associated with death. These are some expenses that can be expected:

- Funeral expenses
- Accounting services
- Legal fees
- Estate and gift taxes

- Executors fees
- Probate court
- Medical fees
- Appraisal fees

Estate planning tools

There are four basic tools that you can use to accomplish the goals and objectives of what you consider to be God's plan of stewardship for your estate. There are many, many tools beyond these four, but if these are implemented then you will have a base from which you can work for more complex planning.

1. A Last Will and Testament

A will is a legal document that expresses your wishes regarding who will take care of your family and how you want your possessions and assets to be distributed at your death. Your loved ones are the primary reasons for having a valid will. A will leaves your property to specifically named individuals known as "beneficiaries." The property transferred based on the terms of the will is known as a "bequest."

2. Revocable Living Trust

A Revocable Living Trust (RLT) is a preferred estate-planning alternative that empowers the family, friends and/or ministries to be at the center and in control of wealth transfer while avoiding many negative tax consequences. When a RLT is funded and combined with a will and

---

NOTES

191

durable power of attorney, it has the following advantages: 1) it is difficult to contend by the court; 2) it holds title to assets before your death (unlike a will) 3) it can be used to avoid probate for 100% of your property; 4) it is confidential and therefore preserves privacy; 5) it provides safety in cases of mental or physical disability; 6) it increases estate liquidity and mobility; and 7) it avoids estate taxes in most cases; 8) it can be easily amended.

Revocable living trusts always require a trustee. This role may be filled by individuals or entities (such as banks or trust companies). A trusted friend or family member may be a likely candidate to act on behalf of the grantor (the deceased) and for the benefit of the beneficiaries, but they should have financial knowledge. A trustee has a set of specific duties relative to the financial aspects of managing the estate, which are different from the duties of an executor, but the same person can fill both roles.

Corporate trustees are well equipped to serve the role of trustee. They don't move, have experience, have investment expertise, have accounting ability, can keep assets safe, are objective, and are less likely to be accused or criticized for not exercising integrity. The disadvantage is that they charge fees, and may not provide as much personal attention. However, in my experience, the cost of the fees far outweighs the risk to harming family relationships.

3. Durable Power of Attorney

The realities of life dictate that we must consider naming someone to

---

NOTES

manage our property in case of mental or physical disability prior to death. You may want to grant the power to manage your property in case of disability to an individual or a bank trust department. This is called a *Durable Power of Attorney for Disability.*

A separate power of attorney can be granted to an individual to make decisions relating to health care during disability. This power should be granted to an individual whom you trust to hold your personal care and well being as a priority. It is called a *Durable Power of Attorney for Health Care.* Without this instrument, a court would have to intervene, which can be costly and time-consuming.

4. Living Will

This document states your wishes about how life-prolonging treatment is provided or withheld if you cannot communicate your wishes for yourself. A living will, or health care directive, tells your family and doctors what you want done in certain medical situations. This document is written up when you are competent and of sound mind, and is in conjunction with your Durable Power of Attorney for Health Care. You can revoke this authority at any time.

An Introduction to Wills

Life is very unpredictable and God's timetable may be very different than we expect. As important as wills are, it is estimated that seven out of ten Americans die without a valid one. If you have ever had to deal with the problems left by a family member or friend who died without a will, you know that

NOTES

the time, effort, and expense are well worth it. Each state has very strict laws regulating the execution and validity of a will. Be sure to have competent legal counsel familiar with the laws of your state draft it.

Wills and Probate. Wills are public documents and do not avoid the probate process. At the death of the will-maker, the will is filed with the county probate court and can be viewed by the public. Probate is the period of time where the deceased person's estate is administered under the supervision of the probate court. During probate the will is "proved" and claims against the estate are heard. Without a will, the legislature of the state where the deceased resides determines distribution based on an established set of guidelines in that state.

Wills won't always transfer property. Joint tenancy ownership (husband and wife) automatically dictates that the surviving tenant becomes the legal owner of the asset regardless of what the will says. Likewise, life insurance proceeds, retirement plans, annuities, and other asset accounts are transferred outside of the will by beneficiary forms. Therefore, your will may or may not transfer a sizeable part of your estate, and it is important to know what assets are and are not affected by your will.

Wills are effective only at death. Wills are ineffective for disability planning because they do not hold title to property, cannot distribute assets to you in the event of disability, and cannot empower someone to manage your assets for you during your lifetime. Because a will takes effect only at death, it offers no lifetime benefits.

NOTES

Wills are changeable. Prior to your death, your will is revocable. It can be amended, altered, or revoked a number of times. Wills are revised by the use of codicils, which are short amendments making simple changes. Or you can revoke an existing will by writing a new one. At death the will become unchangeable. The following list of possible life circumstances could necessitate revisions to your will: changes in family or friends, financial changes, availability of or lack of interest by your personal representative, a move to another state, guardian issues, desire to make a bequest to a new, different, or additional ministry.

What Else can be Accomplished with a Will?

- A will should include a final written testimony proclaiming your faith in Christ and encouraging your loved ones to put their faith in Him. This can be the most significant message you leave your family and a great way to transfer your values.
- Pay debts and expenses related to your final illness.
- Authorize payment of taxes.
- Transfer personal property according to your desires.
- Make distributions to family members and/or ministry organizations, and distribute the remainder of your estate (non-specified distributions) to individuals/ministries.
- Nominate guardians of minor children or incompetent individuals.
- Establish trusts for the benefit of minor children or other individuals for whom you have income responsibilities.

NOTES

- Name the trustee of your revocable living trust or charitable trust, and empower the trustee to carry out the terms of the trusts.
- Fulfill waive bond requirements for your personal representative and simplify probate and reduce expenses. A bond can be equal to 10% of estate value.

What if I Die Without a Will?

- Your property distributions will occur according to the laws of the state.
- Your estate will be managed by court-appointed administrators who may be people that you have never met.
- Those people who mean the most to you may not benefit.
- No gift will be made to support ministries you love.
- Your heirs may have to wade through a host of legalities that a will could have avoided.
- Your state laws may block your spouse from inheriting your entire estate, but divide it equally among your children and spouse.
- Administration expenses and taxes may be greater.
- Your family business may be negatively affected or even have to be dissolved.

Every estate should name an executor (or personal representative) who will act on the directives that you have set forth in your written will or estate plan. An executor should be chosen using the following guidelines:

- Always name a prime candidate and one or more alternates willing to serve.
- Seriously consider someone other than your children if there is any potential for family conflict. Be sure to discuss it with them before making it final.
- Name someone who is healthy and likely to outlive you.

NOTES

- Decide whether co-executors have authority to act independently of each other, or if consensus is required.

Specific executor duties and responsibilities are defined by state law, and are mostly routine. When the will is drafted well, the probate attorney handles all of the legal details. However, it is a good idea to have an awareness of the basic duties of an executor so that you will know what you are asking when you name an executor for your estate. Executors have the basic responsibility to make sure that what you said in your will actually occurs. So, if your will says that Suzie gets the antique dresser, then the executor makes sure that Suzie and the dresser connect.

Specifically, an executor will:
- Check in with the probate attorney and sign legal papers.
- Learn about your property.
- Account for and determine the fair market value of all assets and liabilities.
- Prepare the final federal and state individual income tax returns.
- Pay final bills and any death taxes (using estate funds).
- Make sure all property goes to the people and/or organizations as described in the will.
- Obtain copies of the death certificate and locate beneficiaries.
- Examine and inventory your safe deposit box if you have one.
- Collect mail and cancel credit cards.
- Notify the Social Security Administration of your death.
- Release bank account funds covered by your will.

NOTES

Your executor is called a "fiduciary," which means they must act in good faith. Executors are legally entitled to be paid from your estate for doing their job. The fee ranges from a pre-determined percentage of the probated estate to "reasonable compensation." In reality, an executor will often waive the fees, especially if they inherit part of your estate. However, this is something that you may want to discuss with your executor prior to making a final decision or agreement.

Common Estate Planning Mistakes

Many mistakes can be made during the complex process of estate planning. Some of the most common errors include:

1. Not writing a will. Without a will you lose control of your estate, the expense of administering it increases, and the inheritance to your heirs decreases.

2. Failure to update a will. As family and financial circumstances change, and your understanding of important stewardship principles increases, your will may need to be updated. Review your will at least every 2-3 years to determine if any changes are needed. But, it is best to review it every year.

3. Inaccurate or poor record keeping. If you don't have accurate records of your finances and possessions while you are creating your estate plan, you will likely omit some items or miscalculate values. Furthermore, if your executor and/or trustee can't decipher your records after your death, it will be very difficult to fulfill your wishes.

NOTES

4. Making an inadequate estate plan. Sometimes a simple will is not enough, and a Revocable Living Trust (RLT) or other trust tool is needed to avoid/reduce taxes upon the death of the second spouse. For estates over $1,000,000, both spouses should consider more than just a simple will. The laws are changing and this figure will increase to 3.5 million by the year 2009.

5. Failure to monitor estate growth. Your planning should allow for estate growth. Even though your estate is below $1 million today, with inflation, savings and investment growth, it can exceed that in a very short time. Plan accordingly.

6. Inaccurate estate valuation. Many people underestimate the value of their estate because they are not aware of what is included. Death benefits from life insurance policies, personal property, and retirement plans are all part of your estate values.

7. Lack of liquidity. Estates may not include assets that are easily converted into cash. This could cause a problem if cash is needed to pay taxes, funeral costs, etc. Life insurance may be purchased to provide funds to pay these expenses.

8. No plans to transfer your business. A common oversight of business owners is to not plan for continued operation of their business upon their death. Little or no planning can create a much greater tax burden.

9. Poor choice of executor or guardian. The responsibilities of the executor

---

NOTES

---

and or guardian can be time consuming. Many times individuals who are chosen are not willing or able to devote the necessary time. When selecting these people, look both at their competence and willingness to serve.

10. Not "funding" a revocable living trust. Assets must be titled/re-titled to the trust to escape probate. The trust becomes the actual owner and the grantor of the trust retains control during his or her lifetime. Not "funding" or transferring title makes a trust an ineffective estate planning tool.

In Summary: Steps for Estate Planning

Doing the work of an estate plan is a worthy exercise. After all, you have worked through the concepts and worksheets in this book to learn how to achieve financial freedom. Taking these additional needed steps to secure and transfer your assets against the pitfalls of poor planning, or none at all, will give you a peace of mind and be a great help to your family after your death.

A lot has been covered in this chapter. Hopefully, the list below will give you a clear summary of steps to take to start properly managing your estate.

1. Determine the priorities of your estate plan. Do you want to create a steady income for life to provide for yourself, your spouse and your dependent children, transfer belongings and assets to family and friends, set up education accounts, bless a ministry or organization, a combination of these things, or something else?

2. Organize your financial records. Gather and keep information on your

---

NOTES

financial advisors, employment data, bank accounts, insurance records, investment data, tax returns, wills, deeds, and titles to any property you own or are paying for. Keep all records in a safe and accessible place.

3. Educate yourself. It is helpful to read magazines and books on financial planning and attend seminars. These can give you new and better ways to take care of all God has entrusted to you. The Internet is becoming a very useful source for information and can assist you in the education process. There is a list of words and phrases at the end of the chapter to help you search the Web.

4. Choose a financial advisor(s). This can include an attorney, CPA, insurance agent and financial planner. Sometimes churches have financial planners on staff who work with individuals for a fee or as a service to the Lord.

5. Preserve your estate. Look at all options for increasing, using, preserving, and transferring your estate assets. Consider tax-advantage vehicles that may be available to you like 401(k)s, 403(b)s, IRAs or other tax-deferred growth opportunities. There are also many charitable trusts and annuities and other gift tools that can be used to create income, receive tax deductions, and transfer assets.

6. Formulate a plan and put the plan in action. Everyone will have an estate plan at death. You can write it yourself, or you can allow the state to make it for you. The estate plan you write is the only one that will distribute your assets according to your wishes, so review and revise it on a regular basis. It is best to do this on a yearly basis or when major changes are make (like another child, purchasing more investments, etc.)

NOTES

7. Review and revise your plans and documents on a regular basis. It is best to do this yearly or when major changes occur in your life circumstances (such as having another baby, changing your investment strategies, changing your giving priorities, etc.)

Successful estate planning includes the development of a long-term stewardship program that proactively manages personal and business assets. A critical component of living in financial freedom is fulfilling your stewardship responsibilities, including careful and thorough will and estate planning.

More and more families are recognizing the importance and value of estate and will planning and they are making it a higher priority. You have the opportunity to discover God's overall plan of stewardship for your life and family. Through an effective estate plan, you can make decisions today that will positively impact many lives in the future to the glory of God.

NOTES

For Application

Personal Finance Improvement Checklist

____ Stop procrastinating and write that will.

____ Begin your education through books and the Internet. Use the list below to help direct your search.

Estate Planning Words

- Biblical Stewardship
- Estate Stewardship
- Estate Planning
- Will Planning
- Last Will and Testament
- Will
- Living Will
- Power of Attorney
- Estate Probate
- Planned Giving
- Revocable Living Trust
- Charitable Trust
- Charitable Gift Annuity
- Estate Taxes
- Estate Planning Attorney

____ Find a professional to assist you with your estate planning needs. Consider an organization that will understand your Christian beliefs and stewardship motivations.

____ Communicate your stewardship desires to your family, even though it may be uncomfortable. Solicit their feedback.

____ Consider showing your love for the Lord with a charitable gift through a bequest in your will.

____ Eliminate excuses for not planning for the use and distribution of your estate assets.

____ Consider the advantages of a Revocable Living Trust.

Reflections on Estate Planning

1. Does your estate plan reflect your faith? Have you considered stewardship principles in your planning? If not, maybe now is the time to review your estate plan to be sure that your assets are used to glorify God after your death.

2. How has this chapter affected your perception of estate planning? Do you see how this issue applies to everyone who has responsibility for any amount of possessions? What do you think about the suggestion that it is a spiritual issue and should be a steward-ship priority for the Christian? Read Matthew 24:45-51 and Matthew 25:14-30. These speak of proper management and preparedness because we don't know what will hap-pen in the future. Write your thoughts about stewardship in this area below.

   _____

   _____

   _____

3. Carefully consider your motives for building and managing your estate. If your intent is to gain wealth for wealth's sake, read Ecclesiastes 5:10-12, which describes the folly of this position. What have your motivations for the future been? If you have had no plan, what personal reflection has your reading of this chapter caused?

   _____

   _____

   _____

4. The primary focus of estate planning should be to provide for our family and to pre-serve relationships. Ecclesiastes 5:13-14 describes the effects of poor estate manage-ment. Note the great grief that there is no inheritance for the son. This corresponds to I Timothy 5:8, which admonishes us to provide for our family. What actions do you need to take to get on the path of better management so that you can provide for your family? _____

   _____

   _____

5. As stewards, we manage what God owns, and He expects a maximum return on invest-ment. Notice in Luke 16:1-9 how he praises the shrewd manager. The word shrewd is a synonym for astute, insightful, and perceptive. This "shrewd management" must rely on the biblical principles found in Matthew 7:24-27 and Psalm 127:1. What would you

do differently today to be praised by the Master as a shrewd manager of the estate that He has entrusted to you? Is your foundation built on Him?

_____

_____

_____

6. Additional Scriptures for review and reflection:
   Proverbs 13:22 and 24:3-4, Jeremiah 29:11, Ecclesiastes 5:19-20, Luke 12:13-21, and Romans 8:38

Prayer:

Lord, thank you for giving us your wisdom through scripture. I confess that I have not considered estate planning as a spiritual and stewardship responsibility in the past, but I have learned that I am a steward of the things that you have put into my care. As your servant I want to be a shrewd manager of your affairs so that I can be worthy of your praise. If my motives for building up and managing assets are wrong, please identify those to me because I now know that my purpose is to provide for my family and to honor you with my wealth. Thank you for showing me through the lessons in this book that financial freedom is a condition of the heart in relationship to you more than it is being debt free. Amen.

CONCLUSION

Now What?

We have covered a lot of material in these eight chapters. By now, you have probably learned some new things, have been reminded of some old things, as well as experienced some "ah-ha's" along the way. You may be feeling like you need to categorize all this information into a list of next steps so that you can begin to put it to use in your journey toward financial freedom.

We'll discuss some potential next steps in a moment, but first it seems that it would be helpful to record your thoughts and attitudes toward the topic of financial freedom. Has your concept changed since you picked up this book? What does financial freedom look like to you now? How does this view impact your spiritual perspective of finances and stewardship? Is financial freedom as much a spiritual journey as a financial one?

Before you review the Next Action Steps below you will want to have a grasp of these answers so that you can map out an action plan that fits your own objectives. As you think through the questions above, write a definition of financial freedom as it applies to you in the section below:

_____

_____

_____

_____

_____

_____

_____

_____

_____

_____

Next Action Steps:

1. Pray for guidance, wisdom, and direction as you begin to develop a plan for your financial future.

2. Gather your financial information together and complete the Debt Reduction Worksheet in chapter five, the Household Budget Worksheet in chapter three, and the Calculating Your Net Worth worksheet in chapter three.

3. The information from these worksheets can help you establish some goals for spending, saving, debt management, and retirement. Use the Goal Planning Worksheet in chapter three as a guide.

4. Review the Personal Finance Improvement Checklists at the end of each chapter and begin a list of action steps for each chapter topic that is applicable to your goals and situation.

5. Evaluate the examples that you are setting for your children. What do you need to put into place or change to improve their learning experiences about financial management and stewardship?

6. Look at your current tithing and giving activities. Are they sporadic, regular, or non-existent? Is there more that you want or need to do in these areas? Ask God for His help as you resolve today to trust Him in your decisions to give to His work.

7. Begin a serious review of retirement and estate planning. These are your lasting legacy to your family and your faith.

8. Start Today!

These action steps will help you get started in your own process on this journey. As you develop your plan, remember to include your spouse in the process. Remain sensitive to the Holy Spirit's leading because keeping your attitudes about stewardship and money in check is a lifelong process. And always remember -- financial freedom is *so much* more than being debt free!